The Drama of Love and Death

A Study of Human Evolution and Transfiguration

Edward Carpenter

Alpha Editions

This edition published in 2021

ISBN : 9789355343758

Design and Setting By
Alpha Editions
www.alphaedis.com
Email - info@alphaedis.com

CHAPTER I

INTRODUCTORY

LOVE and Death move through this world of ours like things apart—underrunning it truly, and everywhere present, yet seeming to belong to some other mode of existence. When Death comes, breaking into the circle of our friends, words fail us, our mental machinery ceases to operate, all our little stores of wit and wisdom, our maxims, our mottoes, accumulated from daily experience, evaporate and are of no avail. These things do not seem to touch or illuminate in any effective way the strange vast Presence whose wings darken the world for us. And with Love, though in an opposite sense, it is the same. Words are of no use, all our philosophy fails—whether to account for the pain, or to fortify against the glamour, or to describe the glory of the experience.

These figures, Love and Death, move through the world, like closest friends indeed, never far separate, and together dominating it in a kind of triumphant superiority; and yet like bitterest enemies, dogging each other's footsteps, undoing each other's work, fighting for the bodies and souls of mankind.

Is it possible that at length and after ages we may attain to liberate ourselves from their overlordship—to dominate *them* and make them our ministers and attendants? Can we wrest them from their seeming tyranny over the human race, and from their hostility to each other? Can we persuade them to lay aside their disguise and appear to us for what they no doubt are—even the angels and messengers of a new order of existence?

It is a great and difficult enterprise. Yet it is one, I think, which we of this generation cannot avoid. We can no longer turn our faces away from Death, and make as if we did not perceive his presence or hear his challenge. This age, which is learning to look the facts of Nature steadily in the face, and see *through* them, must also learn to face this ultimate fact and look through it. And it will surely—and perhaps only—be by allying ourselves to Love that we shall be able to do so—that we shall succeed in our endeavor.

For after all it is not in the main on account of ourselves that we cherish a grudge against the 'common enemy' and dispute his authority, but for the sake of those we love. For ourselves we may be indifferent or acquiescent; but somehow for those others, for those divine ones who have taken our hearts into their keeping, we resent the idea that *they* can perish. We refuse to entertain the thought. Love in some mysterious way forbids the fear of death. Whether it be Siegfried who tramples the flaming, circle underfoot, or the Prince of Heaven who breaks his way through the enchanted thicket, or Orpheus who reaches his Eurydice even in the jaws of hell, or Hercules who wrestles with the lord of the underworld for Alcestis—the ancient instinct of mankind has declared in no uncertain tone that in this last encounter Love must vanquish.

It is in the name, then, of one of these gods that we challenge the other. And yet not without gratitude to both. For it is Azrael's invasion of our world, it is his challenge to *us*, that (perhaps more than anything else) rivets our loyalty to each other. It is his frown that wakes friendship in human souls and causes them to tighten the bonds of mutual devotion. In some strange way these two, though seeming enemies, play into each other's hands; each holds the secret of the other, and between them they conceal a kindred life and some common intimate relation. We feel this in our inmost intuitions; we perceive it in our daily survey of human affairs; and we find it illustrated (as I shall presently point out) in general biology and the life-histories of the most primitive cells. The theme, in fact, of the interplay of Love and Death will run like a thread-motive through this book—not without some illumination, as I would hope, cast by each upon the other, and by both upon our human destiny.

CHAPTER II

THE BEGINNINGS OF LOVE

As I have just suggested, the great human problems of Love and Death are strangely and remarkably illustrated in the most primitive forms of life; and I shall consequently make no apology for detaining the reader for a few moments over modern investigations into the subjects of cell-growth, reproduction and death. If this chapter is a little technical and complex in places, still it may be worth while delaying over it, and granting it some patient consideration, on account of the curious light the study throws on the rest of the book and the general questions therein discussed.

Love seems to be primarily (and perhaps ultimately) an interchange of essences. The Protozoa—those earliest cells, the progenitors of the whole animal and vegetable kingdom—grow by feeding on the minute particles which they find in the fluid surrounding them. The growth continues, till ultimately, reaching the limit of convenient size, a cell divides into two or more portions; and so reproduces itself. The descendant cells or portions so thrown off are simply continuations, by division, of the life of the original or parent cell—so that it has not unfrequently been said that, in a sense, these Protozoa are immortal, since their life continues indefinitely (with branching but without break) from generation to generation. This form of reproduction by simple budding or division extends even up into the higher types of life, where it is sometimes found side by side with the later sexual form of reproduction, as in the case of so-called *parthenogenesis* among insects. It is indeed a kind of virgin-birth; and is well illustrated in the vegetable world by the budding of bulbs, or by the fact that a twig torn from a shrub and placed in the ground will commonly grow and continue the life of the parent plant; or in the lower stages of the animal world, where, among many of the worms, insects, sponges, &c., the life may similarly be continued by division, or by the extrusion of a bud or an egg, without any sex-contact or sex-action whatever.

This seems in fact to be the original and primitive form of generation; and it obviously depends upon *growth*. Generation is the superfluity, the ὕβϱις, of growth, and connects itself in the first instance with the satisfaction of hunger. First hunger, then growth, then reproduction by division or budding. And this process may go on apparently for many generations without change—in the case of certain Protozoa even to hundreds of generations. But a time comes when the growth-power and energy decay, and the vitality diminishes[1]—at any rate, as a rule.[2] But then a variation occurs. Two cells unite, exchange fluids, and part again. It is a new form of nourishment; it is the earliest form of Love. It is a very intimate form of nourishment; for it appears that in general the nuclei themselves of the two cells are shared and in part exchanged. And the vitality so obtained gives the cells a new lease of life. They are in fact regenerated. And each partner grows again actively and reproduces itself by budding and division as before. Sometimes the two uniting cells will remain conjoined; and the joint cell will then generate buds, or in some cases enlarge to bursting point, and so, perishing itself, break up into a numerous progeny.[3]

So far there seems to be but little differentiation between Hunger and Love. Love is only a special hunger which leads cells to obtain nourishment from other cells of the same species; and generation or reproduction in these early stages, being an inevitable accompaniment of growth, follows on the satisfaction of love just as it follows on the satisfaction of hunger. Rolph's words on the relation of these two impulses (quoted by Geddes and Thompson) are very suggestive. He says:—"Conjugation occurs when nutrition is diminished.... It is a necessity for satisfaction, a growing hunger, which drives the animal to engulf its neighbor, to 'isophagy.' The process of conjugation is only a special form of nutrition, which occurs on a reduction of the nutritive income, or an increase of the nutritive needs."

And so far there is no distinction of sex. It is true there may be sex in the sense of union or fusion between two individuals; but there is no distinction of sex, in the sense of male and female. In the Protozoa generally there is simple union or conjugation between cells, which, as far as can be observed, are quite similar to each other. It is a union between similars; and it leads to growth and reproduction. But both union and reproduction at this early stage exist quite independently of any distinctive sex-action, or any differentiation of individuals into male and female.

At a later period, however, Sex comes in. It is obvious that for growth (and reproduction) two things are necessary, which are in some degree antagonistic to each other—on the one hand the pursuit and capture of food, which means *activity* and force, and on the other hand the digestion and assimilation of the food, which means *quiescence* and passivity. And it seems that at a certain stage—in general, when "animals" have already been formed by the conjunction of many protozoic cells in co-operative colonies—this differentiation sets in, and some individuals specialize towards activity and the chase, while others (of the same species) specialize towards repose and assimilation. The two sets of qualities are clearly only useful in combination with each other, and yet, as I have said, they are to some degree contrary to each other; and therefore it is quite natural that the two corresponding groups of individuals should form two great branches in each race, diverse yet united.

These two branches are the male and female—the active, energy-spending, hungry, food-obtaining branch; and the sessile, non-active, assimilative and reproductive branch. And by the division of labor consequent on the formation of these two branches the whole race is benefited; but only of course on condition that the diverse elements are reunited from time to time. It is in the fusion of these elements that the real quality and character of the race is restored; and it is by their fusion that development and reproduction are secured.

In some of the Infusorians[4] there seems to be a beginning of sex-differentiation, and fusion takes place between two individuals slightly differing from each other; but as we have already seen, in most of the Protozoa the union is a union of *similars*—that is, as far as can at present be observed, though of course there is a great probability that here also there is generally *some* difference which supplies the attraction and the value of union.[5]

It is in the *Metazoa* generally, and those forms of life which consist of co-operative *colonies* of cells, that sex-differentiation into male and female begins to decisively assert itself. Here—since it is obviously impossible for all the cells of one individual to fuse with all the cells of another—certain special cells are set apart in each organism for the purpose of union or conjugation; and it seems quite natural that in the course of time the differentiation spoken of above, into male and female, should set in—each individual tending to become decisively either masculine or feminine—both in the sex-cells or sex-apparatus, and (though in a less marked degree) in the general 'body' and structure.

In the lower forms of life, generally, as among the amphibia, fishes, molluscs, &c., the male and female sex-cells—the sperm and the germ—do not conjugate within either of the parent bodies, but are expelled from each, in order to meet and fuse in some surrounding medium, like water. There the double cell, so formed, develops into the new individual. But in higher forms the meeting takes place, and the first stages of development ensue, *within* one of the bodies. And, as one might expect, this occurs within the body of the female. For the female, as we have said, represents quiescence, growth, assimilation. The germ or ovum is large compared with the spermatozoon; it is also sessile in habit. The spermatozoon, on the other hand, is exceedingly active. And so it seems natural that the latter should seek out the germ within the body of the female. Just as, in general, the female animal remains impassive and quiescent, and is sought out by the male, so the female germ remains at home within the female body, and receives its visitor or visitors there. And the whole apparatus of connection is symbolical of this relation. The body of the female is the temple in which the sacred mystery of the union or fusion of two individuals is completed, as a means to the birth or creation of a new individual.

Yet though the female is thus privileged to be the receptacle and sanctum of the life-giving power, it must not be thought that this argues superiority of the female, as such, over the male. The process of conjunction is sometimes spoken of as a fertilization merely, implying the idea that the ovum or female element is the main thing, and that *this* only requires a slight impulse or stimulus from the male side for its powers of development to be started and set in operation. But though it is true that the ovum can in many cases of the lower forms of life be started developing by the administration of a chemical solution or even a mechanical needle-prick, this development does not seem to continue; and modern investigation shows that in normal fecundation an absolute equality reigns, as far as we can see, between the two contracting parties and their contributions to the new being that has to be formed.

Nothing is more astounding than the results of these investigations; and they not only show us that the protozoic cells (and sex-cells), instead of being very simple in structure, are already extremely complex, and that their changes in the act of fertilization or fusion are *strangely elaborate and systematic*; but they suggest that though to us these cells may represent the microscopic beginnings of life in its most primitive stages, in reality they stand for the first visible results of long antecedent operations, and indicate highly organized and, we may say, intelligent forces at work within them.

The mere process by which a primitive cell divides and reproduces itself has an air of demonic intelligence about it. Roughly, the process may be described as follows. The nucleus appears to be the most important portion of a cell. Certainly it is so as regards the supply of hereditary and formative material—the surrounding protoplasm fulfilling more of a nutritive and protective function. Within and through the liquid of the nucleus there spreads an irregular network of a substance which is (for a purely accidental reason) called *chromatin*. As long as the nucleus is at rest, this network is fairly evenly distributed through it; but the first oncoming of division is signalled by the break-up of the chromatin into a limited and definite number of short, threadlike bodies—to which the name *chromosomes* has been given. These *chromosomes*, after some curious evolutions, finally arrange themselves in a line across the middle of the nucleus; and they are apparently governed in this operation, and the whole splitting of the cell is governed, by a minute, starlike and radiating centre (called *centrosome*), which first appearing outside the nucleus and in the general protoplasm of the cell, seems to play a dominant part in the whole process. This *centrosome*, when the time comes for the cell-division, itself divides in two, and the two starlike centres so formed (which are to become *centrosomes* of the two new cells), slowly move to opposite ends or poles of the original cell—all the time, as they do so, throwing out raylike threads or fibrils which connect them somehow with the chromosomes and which seem to regulate the movements of the latter, till, as described, the latter form themselves in a line across the centre of the cell, transversely to the line joining the poles. At this stage, then, we have a tiny, starlike centrosome at each end of the cell, and a transverse line of chromosomes between. (Also, during the process the wall or enclosing membrane of the nucleus has disappeared and the general contents of cell and nucleus have become undivided.) It is at this moment that the real division begins. The chromosomes—of which it is said that there are always a definite and invariable number for every species of plant or animal,[6] and which are now generally supposed to contain the hereditary elements or determinants of the future individual—these chromosomes have already arranged themselves longitudinally and end-on to each other across the middle of the cell. They now, apparently under the influence of the radiating points at each pole, split longitudinally (as one splits a log of wood)—so that each chromosome, dividing throughout its length, contributes one half of itself to one pole and one half to the other. The halves so formed separate, and approach their respective poles; and at the same time the cell-wall constricting itself along the equatorial line, or line of separation, soon divides the original cell into two. Meanwhile the chromosomes in each new division group themselves (not round but) near their respective poles or centrosomes, and a new nucleus membrane forming, encloses each group, so that finally we have two cells of exactly the same constitution as the original one, and with exactly the same number and quality of chromosomes as the original.[7]

The whole process seems very strange and wonderful. No military evolutions and formations, no complex and mystic dance of initiates in a temple, with advances and retreats, and combinations and separations, and exchanges of partners, could seem more fraught with intelligence.[8] Yet this is what takes place among some of the very lowest forms of life, on the division of a single cell into two. And it is exactly the same, apparently, which takes place in the higher forms of life when the single cell which is the result of the fusion together of the sperm-cell and the germ-cell, divides and subdivides to form the 'body' of the creature. As is well known, the joint cell divides first into two; then each of the cells so formed divides into two, making four in all; then each of these divides into two, making eight; then each into two again, making 16, 32, 64, and so on—till they number the thousands, hundreds of thousands, millions, which in effect build up and constitute the body. And at each division the process is carried out with this amazing care and exactness of partition described—so that every cell is verily continuous and of the same nature with the original cell, and contains the same nuclear elements, derived half from the father and half from the mother. Yet in the process a differentiation has set in, so that in the end each cell becomes so far modified as to be adapted for its special position and function in the body—for the skin, mucous membrane, blood corpuscles, brain, muscular tissue, and so forth.[9] It is worth while looking carefully at the body of an animal, or one's own body, in order to realize what this means—to realize that the entire creature, in all its form and feature, its coloring, marking, swiftness of limb, complexity of brain, and so on, has provably been exhaled from a single cell, *is* indeed that original cell with its latent powers and virtue made manifest; and to remember that that original cell was itself the fusion of two parent cells, the male and the female.

A word, then, upon this matter of the fusion of the two parent cells in one. Here, again, two very remarkable things appear. One refers to the equality of the sexes; the other refers to the onesidedness (or deficiency or imperfection) which seems to be the characteristic *and* the motive power of the phenomenon of sex.

With regard to the first point, we saw that among the Protozoa conjugation occurs for the most part between two individual cells which are alike in size and (to all appearance) alike in constitution; and this conjugation leads to reproduction. But when among the higher forms sex begins to show, the conjugating cells—sperm-cell and germ-cell—are generally unlike in size, and often in the higher animals extremely unlike—as in the human *spermatozoon* and *ovum*, of which the latter is a thousand times the volume of the former;[10] and this has sometimes led, as remarked before, to an exaggerated view of the preponderant importance of one sex. But the curious fact seems to be that when the spermatozoon of the human or higher animal penetrates the ovum, there is a preliminary period before its nucleus actually combines with the nucleus of the ovum, during which the nucleus rapidly absorbs nourishment from the surrounding protoplasm, and *grows*—grows till it becomes of *exactly the same size* as the nucleus of the ovum. The situation then is that there are two nuclei of the same size and both charged with chromatin of the same general character, in close proximity, and waiting to fuse with each other.

The product of that fusion is a new being; and as far as can at present apparently be observed, the parts played by the two sexes in the process are quite equal. There may be *difference* of function but there is no inequality. "Both male and female cells," says Professor Rolleston,[11] "prepare themselves for conjugation long before it takes place, and neither of them can be said to be a more active agent in fertilization than the other. Not 'fertilization' but 'fusion' is the keyword of the process. The mystical conception, as old as Plato, of the male and female as representing respectively the two halves of a complete being, turns out to be no poetic metaphor. As regards the essential features of reproduction, it is a literal fact."

The second remarkable point has to do with the onesidedness of sexual conjugation, and the complementary nature of the exchange involved. This is truly noteworthy and interesting. It is evident that if the sperm-cell and germ-cell simply coalesced, containing each the amount of chromatin characteristic of the species—say sixteen chromosomes in the case of the human being—the result would be a cell with double the proper amount, *say thirty-two chromosomes*, i.e. *an amount belonging to another species*. "What happens is that each of the reproductive cells, male and female, prepares itself for conjugation *by getting rid of half its* chromosomes. Two divisions of the nucleus take place, *not* as in the ordinary fashion of cell-division, when the chromosomes split longitudinally, but in such a way that, in each division, four of the sixteen chromosomes (making eight in all) are bodily expelled from the nucleus and from the cell, when they either perish, or, in some cases, appear to help in forming an envelope of nutritive matter round the germ-cell. These divisions are called 'maturation divisions,' and until they are accomplished fecundation is impossible."[12] Thus the two nuclei, having each their number of chromosomes reduced to half the normal number (in this case to eight), are now ready to coalesce and so form a new cell with the proper number belonging to the species (*i.e.* sixteen). This cell is the commencement of the new being, and, as already described, it divides and re-divides, and the innumerable cells so formed differentiate themselves into different tissues, until the whole animal is built up.

Says Professor E. B. Wilson:—"The one fact of maturation that stands out with perfect clearness and certainty amid all the controversies surrounding it, is a reduction of the *number of chromosomes in the ultimate germ [and sperm] cells*[13] to one half the number characteristic of the somatic cells. It is equally clear that this reduction is a preparation of the germ [and sperm] cells for their subsequent union, and a means by which the number of chromosomes is held constant in the species."[14]

This extrusion or expulsion by each of the conjugating cells of half its constituent elements is certainly very strange.[15] And it seems strangely deliberate.[16] Various theories have been formed on the subject, but at present there is apparently no satisfactory conclusion as to what exactly takes place. Some think that in the one case certain male elements are expelled, and in the other case certain female elements; and anyhow it seems probable that a complementary action sets in, by which each prepares itself to supply a different class of elements from the other, thus rendering the conjunction more effectual. Plato has been already quoted with regard to male and female being only the two halves of a complete original being. He also says (in the speech of Socrates in the *Banquet*) that the mother of Love was Poverty, and that Love "possesses thus far his mother's nature that he is ever the companion of Want." And it would appear that in the most primitive grades of life the same is true, and that two cells combine or coalesce in order to mutually supply some want or deficiency.

Anyhow, in the process just described two points stand out pretty clear: first, the exact quality of the number of chromosomes contributed by sperm-cell and germ-cell to the fertilized ovum—which seems to indicate that the descendant being has an equal heredity from each parent[17]—though of course it does not follow that both heredities become equally prominent or manifest in the descendant body; and secondly, that the same is true of all the cells in this new body—that they each contain the potentialities of the joint cell from which they sprang, and therefore the potentialities of both parents.

These amazing conclusions concerning the origins of life and reproduction—here, of course, very briefly and imperfectly presented—cannot but give us pause. Contemplating the evolutions and affinities of these infinitely numerous but infinitely small organisms which build up our visible selves, and the strange intelligence which seems to pervade their movements, the mind reels—somewhat as it does in contemplating the evolutions and affinities of the unimaginable stars.[18] We seem, certainly, to trace the same laws or operations in these minutest regions as we trace in our own corporeal and mental relations. Cells attract each other just as human beings do; and the attraction seems to depend, to a certain degree, on difference. The male spermatozoon seeks the female ovum, just as the male animal, as a rule, seeks and pursues the female. Primitive cells divide and redivide and differentiate themselves, building up the animal body, just in the same way as primitive thoughts and emotions divide and redivide and differentiate themselves, building up the human mind. But though we thus see processes with which we are familiar repeated in infinitesimal miniature, we seem to be no nearer than before to any 'explanation' of them, and we seem to see no promise of any explanation. We merely obtain a larger perspective, and a suggestion that the universal order is of the same character throughout—with a suspicion perhaps that the explanation of these processes does not lie in any concatenation of the things themselves, but in some other plane of being of which these concatenations are an allegory or symbolic expression. In portions of the following chapters I shall trace more in detail the resemblance or parallelism between these processes among the Protozoa and some of our own experiences in the great matters of Life and Love and Death.[19]

CHAPTER III

LOVE AS AN ART

THE astounding revelation of the first great love is a thing which the youthful human being can hardly be prepared for, since indeed it cannot very well be described in advance, or put into terms of reasonable and well-conducted words. To feel—for instance—one's whole internal economy in process of being melted out and removed to a distance, as it were into the keeping of some one else, is in itself a strange physiological or psychological experience—and one difficult to record in properly scientific terms! To lose consciousness never for a moment of the painful void so created—a void and a hunger which permeates all the arteries and organs, and every cranny of the body and the mind, and which seems to rob the organism of its strength, sometimes even to threaten it with ruin; to forego all interest in life, except in one thing—and that thing a person; to be aware, on the other hand, with strange elation and joy, that this new person or presence is infusing itself into one's most intimate being—pervading all the channels, with promise (at least) of marriage and new life to every minutest cell, and causing wonderful upheavals and transformations in tissue and fluids; to find in the mind all objects of perception to be changed and different from what they were before; and to be dimly conscious that the reason why they are so is because the background and constitution of the perceiving mind is itself changed—that, as it were, there is another person beholding them as well as oneself—all this defies description in words, or any possibility of exact statement beforehand; and yet the actual fact when it arrives is overwhelming in solid force and reality. If, besides, to the insurgence of these strange emotions we add—in the earliest stages of love at least—their bewildering fluctuation, from the deeps of vain longing and desire to the confident and ecstatic heights of expectation or fulfilment—the very joys of heaven and pangs of hell in swift and tantalizing alternation—the whole new experience is so extraordinary, so unrelated to ordinary work-a-day life, that to recite it is often only to raise a smile of dismissal of the subject—as it were into the land of dreams.

And yet, as we have indicated, the thing, whatever it is, is certainly by no means insubstantial and unreal. Nothing seems indeed more certain than that in this strange revolution in the relations of two people to each other—called "falling in love"—and behind all the illusions connected with it, *something is happening*, something very real, very important. The falling-in-love may be reciprocal, or it may be onesided; it may be successful, or it may be unsuccessful; it may be only a surface indication of other and very different events; but anyhow, deep down in the sub-conscious world, *something* is happening. It may be that two unseen and only dimly suspected existences are becoming really and permanently united; it may be that for a certain period, or (what perhaps comes to the same thing) that to a certain *depth*, they are transfusing and profoundly modifying each other; it may be that the mingling of elements and the transformation is taking place almost entirely in one person, and only to a slight degree or hardly at all in the other; yet in all these cases—beneath the illusions, the misapprehensions, the mirage and the *maya*, the surface satisfactions and the internal disappointments—something very real is happening, an important growth and evolution is taking place.

To understand this phenomenon in some slight degree, to have some inkling of the points of the compass by which to steer over this exceedingly troubled sea, is, one might say, indispensable for every youthful human creature; but alas! the instruction is not provided—for indeed, as things are to-day, the adult and the mature are themselves without knowledge, and their eyes without speculation on the subject. Treatises on the Art of Love truly exist—and some (for the field they cover) very good ones, like the *Ars Amatoria* of Ovid or the *Kama-sutra* of Vatsayana; but they are concerned mainly or wholly with the details and technicalities of the subject—with the conduct of intrigues and amours, with times and seasons, positions and preparations, unguents and influences. It is like instructions given to a boatman on the minutiæ of his craft—how to contend with wind and wave, how to use sail and oar, to steer, to tack, to luff to a breaker, and so forth; all very good and necessary in their way, but who is there to point us our course over the great Ocean, and the stars by which to direct it? The later works on this great subject—though not despising the more elementary aspects—will no doubt have to proceed much farther, into the deep realms of psychology, biological science, and ultimately of religion.[20]

As we have just said, Love is concerned with growth and evolution. It is—though as yet hardly acknowledged in that connection—a root-factor of ordinary human growth; for in so far as it is a hunger of the individual, the satisfaction of that hunger is necessary for individual growth—necessary (in its various forms) for physical, mental and spiritual nourishment, for health, mental energy, large affectional capacity, and so forth. And it is—though this too is not sufficiently acknowledged—a root-factor of the Evolution process. For in so far as it represents and gives rise to the union of two beings in a new form, it plainly represents a step in Evolution, and plainly suggests that the direction of that step will somehow depend upon the character and quality of the love concerned. Thus the importance, the necessity, of the study of the art of love is forced on our attention. It has to be no longer a subterranean, unrecognized, and even rather disreputable cult, but an openly acknowledged and honorable department of human life, leading in its due time to broad and commonsense instructions and initiations for the young.

Casting a glance back at the love-affairs of the Protozoa, as briefly described in the preceding chapter, there certainly seems to be a kind of naive charm about them. The simple and wholehearted way in which on occasions they fuse with one another, losing or merging completely their own separate individualities in the process; or again part from each other after having exchanged essences in a kind of affectionate cannibalism; the obvious and unconcealed relation between love and hunger; the first beginnings of generation; and the matter-of-fact manner in which one person, when he finds it convenient, divides in half and becomes two persons, and after a time perhaps divides again and becomes four persons, and again and again until he is many thousands or millions—and yet it is impossible to decide (and he himself probably is not quite clear) as to whether he is still one person or different persons—all this cannot fail to excite our admiration and respect, nor to give us, also, considerable food for thought.

One of the first things to strike us, and to suggest an application to human life, is the importance of Love, among these little creatures, for the health of the individual. The authors of *The Evolution of Sex* say in one passage (p.): "Without it [conjugation], the Protozoa, which some have called 'immortal,' die a natural death. Conjugation is the necessary condition of their eternal youth and immortality. Even at this low level, only through the fire of love can the phœnix of the species renew its youth." And again, in another passage (p.), referring to the conclusions of Maupas: "Already we have noted this important result, that conjugation is essential to the health of the species." Thus it appears that, in these primitive stages, fusion more or less complete, or interchange of essences, leads to Regeneration and renewal of vitality—and this long before the distinct phenomena of sex appear. It leads to Regeneration first, and so collaterally, and at a later period, to Generation.

Somehow—though it is not quite clear how—this view of the importance of love to personal health has been sadly obscured in later and Christian times. The dominant Christian attitude converted love, from being an expression and activity of the deepest human life and joy, into being simply a vulgar necessity for the propagation of the species. A violent effort was made to wrench apart the spiritual and corporeal aspects of it. The one aspect was belauded, the other condemned. The first was relegated to heaven, the second was given its *congé* to another place. Corporeal intercourse and the propagation of the race were vile necessities. True affection dwelt in the skies and disdained all earthly contacts. And yet all this was a vain effort to separate what could not be separated. It was like trying to take the pigments out of a picture; to call the picture "good," but the stuff it was painted with "bad."

And so, owing to this denial, owing to this non-recognition of love (in all its aspects) as necessary to personal health, thousands and thousands of men and women through the centuries—some "for the kingdom of heaven's sake," and some for the sake of the conventions of society—have allowed their lives to be maimed and blighted, their health and personal well-being ruined. The deep well-spring and source of human activity and vitality has been desecrated and choked with rubbish. That some sort of purpose, in the evolution of humanity, may have been fulfilled by this strange negation, it would be idle to deny; indeed some such purpose—in view of the wide prevalence of the negation, and its long continuance during the civilization period—seems probable. But this does not in any way controvert the fact that it has in its time caused a disastrous crippling of human health and vitality. Human progress takes place, no doubt, in sections—one foot forward at a time, so to speak; but this does not mean that the other foot can be permanently left in the rear. On the contrary, it means its all the more decided advance when its turn arrives.

To-day we seem at the outset of a new era, and preparing in some way for the rehabilitation of the Pagan conception of the world. The negative Christian dispensation is rapidly approaching its close; the necessity of love in its various forms, as part and parcel of a healthy life, is compelling our attention. No one is so poor a physiognomist as not to recognize the health-giving effects of successful courtship—the heightened color, the brilliant eye, the elastic step; the active brain, the prompt reflexes, the glad outlook on the world. Indeed the effect upon all the tissues—their nourishment, growth, improvement in tone, and so forth—is extraordinary; and yet—remembering what has been said about Love and Hunger—quite natural. For, after all, we have seen that every cell in the body is a *replica* of the original cell from which it sprang; and so the love which reaches one probably in some way reaches all. And there is probably not only union and exchange (in actual intercourse) between two special sex-cells; but there is also (*all through* the period of being "in love") an etheric union and exchange going on between the body-cells generally on each side; and a nourishment of each other by the interchange of finest and subtlest elements.

That this mutual exchange and nutrition may take place between the general cells of two bodies is made all the more probable from the experiments already alluded to with regard to chemical fertilization—whereby it has been shown that some ova or egg-cells may be started on a process of subdivision and growth by treatment with certain chemicals, such as weak solutions of strychnine, or common salt, apart from any fertilization by a spermatozoon.[21] Now since—when the body is once fairly formed—its further growth and sustenance is maintained by continued division and subdivision of the body-cells, this stimulus to growth may easily (we may suppose) be supplied by the subtle radiations and reactions from another body within whose sphere of influence it comes—radiations and reactions sufficiently subtle to pass through the tissues to the various cells, and of course sufficiently characteristic and individual to be in some cases, as we have supposed, highly vitalizing and stimulating—though in other cases of course they may be poisonous and harmful. Of course, also, it is only love that supplies and is the vitalizing relation.

So intense, at times, is this vitalizing force, and so ardent the need of it, that the whole body leaps and throbs in pain. Plato, in his poetic way, explains the scorching sensation in all the skin and tissues by feigning that it is caused by the wing-feathers of the soul sprouting everywhere (*i.e.* according to our view, in every little cell). Nevertheless, his words on the subject are singularly pregnant with meaning. For he says (in the *Phædrus*): "Whenever indeed by gazing on the beauty of the beloved object, and *receiving from that beauty particles which fall and flow in upon it* (and which are therefore called 'desire'), the soul is watered and warmed, it is relieved from its pain, and is glad; but as soon as it is parted from its love, and for lack of that moisture is parched, the mouths of the outlets by which the feathers start become so closed up by drought, that they obstruct the shooting germs; and the germs being thus confined underneath, in company of the desire which has been infused, leap like throbbing arteries, and prick each at the outlet which is closed against it; so that the soul, being stung all over, is frantic with pain."[22]

This fusion of complementaries, then, which is the characteristic of fertilization, takes place between the lovers—not only in respect of their sex-cells, but probably also to a considerable degree in respect of their body-cells. And though with any mortal lovers the complementary nature of the fusion can hardly be so complete as to restore the full glory of the race-life, yet very near to that point it sometimes comes, filling them with mad and immortal-seeming ecstasies, and excusing them indeed for seriously thinking that the wings of their souls have begun to grow! In lesser degree this complementary fusion and exchange is doubtless the explanation (or one explanation) of that very noticeable point—the strange way in which lovers after some years come to resemble each other—in form and feature, in facial expression, tone of voice, carriage of body, handwriting, and all sorts of minute points.

I suppose at this point it will be necessary to explain that the recognition of love (in all its aspects) as a general condition of human health, does not mean a recommendation of wild indulgence in any and every passion—necessary, because in these cases it seems to be generally assumed that the proposer of a very simple thesis means a very great deal more than he says! It is here that the necessity of education comes in; for hitherto public instruction and discussion in these matters have been so defective that folk have been unable to talk about them except in a hysterical way—hysterical on the one side or the other. The *positive* value of love, its positive cultivation as a gracious, superb, and necessary part of our lives has hardly (at least in the Anglo-Saxon world) entered into people's minds. To teach young things to love, and how to love, to actually instruct and encourage them in the art, has seemed something wicked and unspeakable. Says Havelock Ellis:[23] "Whether or not Christianity is to be held responsible, it cannot be doubted that throughout Christendom there has been a lamentable failure to recognize the supreme importance, not only erotically but morally, of the art of love. Even in the great revival of sexual enlightenment now taking place around us there is rarely even the faintest recognition that in sexual enlightenment the one thing essentially necessary is a knowledge of the art of love. For the most part sexual instruction, as at present understood, is purely negative, a mere string of thou-shalt-nots. If that failure were due to the conscious and deliberate recognition that while the art of love must be based on physiological and psychological knowledge, it is far too subtle too complex, too personal, to be formulated in lectures and manuals, it would be reasonable and sound. But it seems to rest entirely on ignorance, indifference, or worse."

It is, I think, not unfair to suppose that it is this indifference or vulgar Philistinism which is largely responsible for the sordid commercialism of the good people of the last century. Finding the lute and the lyre snatched from their hands they were fain to turn to a greater activity with the muck-rake.

Love is a complex of human relations—physical, mental, emotional, spiritual, and so forth—all more or less necessary. And though seldom realized complete, it is felt, and feels itself, to be imperfect without some representation of every side. To limit it to the expression of one particular aspect would be totally inadequate, if not absurd and impossible. A merely physical love, for instance, on the sexual plane, is an absurdity, a dead letter—the enjoyment and fruition of the physical depending so much on the *feeling* expressed, that without the latter there is next to no satisfaction. At best there is merely a negative pleasure, a relief, arising from the solution of a previous state of corporeal tension. And in such cases intercourse is easily followed by depression and disappointment. For if there is not enough of the more subtle and durable elements in love, to remain after the physical has been satisfied, and to hold the two parties close together, why, the last state may well be worse than the first!

But equally absurd is any attempt to limit, for instance, to the mental plane, and to make love a matter of affectionate letter-writing merely, or of concordant views on political economy; or again, to confine it to the emotional plane, and the region of more or less sloppy sentiment; or to the spiritual, with a somewhat lofty contempt of the material—in which case it tends, as hinted before, to become too like trying to paint a picture without the use of pigments. All the phases are necessary, or at least desirable—even if, as already said, a quite complete and all-round relation is seldom realized. The physical is desirable, for many very obvious reasons—including corporeal needs and health, and perhaps especially because it acts in the way of removal of barriers, and *so opens the path* to other intimacies. The mental is desirable, to give form and outline to the relation; the emotional, to provide the something to be expressed; and the spiritual to give permanence and absolute solidity to the whole structure.

It is probably on account of this complex nature that for any big and permanent relationship of this kind there has to be a rather slow and gradual culmination. All the various elements have to be hunted up and brought into line. Like all great ideas love has its two sides—its instantaneous inner side, and its complex outer side of innumerable detail. In *consciousness* it tends to appear in a flash—simple, unique, and unchangeable; but in *experience* it has to be worked out with much labor. *All the elements have to come into operation*, and to contribute their respective quota to the total result. If we remember what happens when the spermatozoon and the ovum coalesce (see ch. ii. p. 19)—the extraordinary changes and disturbances which are induced in the chromatin elements of both nuclei, the fusion of the nuclei, and the ultimate ranging of the chromosomes in a line (for the formation of the new being) in such a way that every element is represented and contributes its share to the process—we cannot but be struck by the strange similarity to our own inner experience: how love searches the heart, drags every element of the inner nature forward from its lurking-place, gives it definition and shape, and somehow insists on it being represented, and, so to speak, toeing the line. We shall return to this point later. Here I only wish to insist on the complexity of the process, in order to show that for any big relationship plenty of time has to be allowed. Whichever side of the nature—mental, emotional, physical, and so forth—may have happened to take the lead, it must not and cannot monopolize the affair. It must drag the other sides in and give them their place. And this means time, and temporary bewilderment and confusion. It is curious how 'falling in love' has this very effect—how it paralyzes for a time—

inhibiting the mental part and even the physical; how the smart talker becomes a dumb ass, and the man about town a modest fool, and the person who always does the right thing seems compelled to do everything wrong—as if a confusion were being created in the mind, analogous to that which we have observed in the cells. When we add to these considerations the extraordinary differences between persons, and between the proportions in which the elements of their characters are mixed, it is obvious how extremely complex the conditions of any one decent love-relation must be, and what tact and patience in the handling it may require.

The ignorance, therefore, which causes a young man, husband or lover, to think that the hurried completion of the sexual act is at once the initiation and the fulfilment of love, is fatal enough. It marks more often the end than the beginning of the affair. For, contrariwise, time and plenty of time has to be given in order to allow the central radiation in each case to have its perfect work. Is it too fanciful to suppose that the *centrosome*, which makes its appearance in the protozoön on its approach to conjunction, and which seems to rule the rearrangement of the chromatin elements within it, is the analogue of the radiating force in human courtship which so strangely sifts out and remoulds the elements of the lover's personality? Does the magic of the centrosome correspond in some sense to the glamour, so well known in human affairs? And do they both proceed from some deep-hidden, profoundly important manifestation of the life, the energy, the divinity if you will, of the Race?

How strange is this matter of the glamour, and its decisiveness in awakening love by its presence, or leaving it cold by absence! Here is a story of a woman who, dreadfully disfigured in countenance by an accident in the hunting-field, called her *fiancé* to her, and nobly offered him his freedom; and he ... accepted it! Accepted it, because, quite really and truly, the destruction of her physical beauty had for him shattered the Vision and the divinity. And here is another similar story where, contrariwise, the man immediately confirmed his love and devotion—because for *him* the glory around her was more illumined by her nobility of feeling than it could be darkened by her bodily defect.

Such glamour, working away in the hidden caverns of being, may at last, like Bruno's "fabro vulcano," weld two souls into one, and bring to light a real, a profound, and perhaps eternal union. It is after all that inner union which is the real thing; which gives all its joys to intercourse, and penetrating down into the world of sense, redeems that world into a thing of glory and beauty. For the complete action of that creative and organizing force plentiful time must be given; and the two lovers must possess their souls in patience till it has had its full and perfect work. Ovid in his *Ars Amatoria* has many lines on this subject. "Let the youth," he says, "with tardy passion burn, like a damp torch" ... "*Non est Veneris properanda voluptas*" ... "*Quod datum ex facili longum male nutrit amorem*" (Love easily granted may not long endure), and so forth. And though these passages no doubt refer mainly to what may be called the practical conduct of amours, yet they have also a very pointed application to the more important aspects of the grand passion. A long foreground of approach, time and tact, diffusion of magnetism, mergence in one another, suffering, and even pain—all these must be expected and allowed for—though the best after all, in this as in other things, is often the unexpected and the unprepared.

And if the man has to allow time for all the elements of his nature to come forward and take their part in the great mystery, all the more is it true that he has to give the woman time for the fulfilling of *her* part. For in general it may be said (though of course with exceptions) that love culminates more slowly in women than in men. Men concentrate obviously on the definite part they have to play; but in women love is more diffused and takes longer to reach the point where it becomes an inspired and creative frenzy of the whole being. Caresses, tendernesses, provocation, sacrifices, and a thousand indirect influences have to gradually conspire to the working out of this result; and not infrequently the situation so arising demands great self-control on the part of the man. Yet these things are worth while. "The real marriage," says some one, "takes place when from their intense love there comes to birth another soul—apart from each, and invisible, yet joining them together, one hand ahold of each—a radiant thing born of the sun and stars, which though tender and fragile at first, grows just like a bodily child, and leads them on, and dances with them."

They are worth while, all these labors and troubles, and delays and sacrifices, if only out of them can be forged a fair and infrangible union. As in all the arts, so in the greatest of the arts, no lasting result can be attained, without such labor. Nor indeed without some degree of pain and suffering. Young folk and inexperienced may think it is not so. They may think that by a lucky stroke and practically without effort a man may write a "Blessed Damozel" or carve in marble a "Greek Slave"; but all experience points differently, and shows that directly or indirectly to such works have gone infinite labor and patience. And so to the conceiving and shaping of a perfect alliance between a man and a woman must always go much of suffering—for it is by suffering that the souls of human beings are brought into form and carved to fitness for each other.

Is it seriously—when one comes to think of it—possible to imagine love without pain? Figure to yourself, O man, a courtship absolutely undenied, from the first accepted, even encouraged, with complaisantly unresisting bride, smiling parents, fair-weather prospects, and cash unlimited! How awfully dull! Does not the stoutest heart quail at the suggestion? Or if such a mating might be deemed pleasant as far as its accessories and conditions were concerned, could it yet be termed Love?

For Love, if worth anything, seems to *demand* pain and strain in order to prove itself, and is not satisfied with an easy attainment. How indeed should one know the great heights except by the rocks and escarpments? And pain often in some strange way seems to be the measure of love—the measure by which we are assured that love is true and real; and so (which is one of the mysteries) it becomes transformed into a great joy. Yes, if men could only understand, here is one of the most precious of the mysteries, and the solving of a great riddle.

But that the course of true love does generally not run smooth is understood, more or less, by every one. And it is woman's strange and imperious instinct—even though at considerable suffering to herself—to see that it *doesn't* run smooth. Ellis practically bases[24] the whole of the evolution of modesty on this instinct—reaching far down in the animal kingdom—by which the female constantly throws difficulties and obstacles in the way of courtship (by her coynesses, contrarieties, changeable moods, and so forth); thus calling out in the male all his ingenuity, his impetuosity, his energy, in overcoming them; rousing dormant elements of his nature; delaying consummation and giving time for his character and all his qualities to concentrate; and indirectly having a like effect upon herself. So that ultimately by this method a maximum of passion and agitation is produced, and in the case of the human being love penetrates to the very deeps and hidden caverns of the soul. Such is the genesis of Modesty—not by any means Nature's *denial* of love, but rather the crafty old dame's method of rendering love, by temporary obstacles, all the more insurgent and irresistible—her method of making it less superficial, of deepening the channels and rendering them more profound.

Practically, and as a matter of policy, a too easy consent to another's love is a mistake. The barb only sticks when the bait is withdrawn. Ovid, it will be remembered, advises that "the lover should be admitted by the *window*, even when the door is quite accessible, and really more convenient";[25] and most girls (though they have not read Ovid) know instinctively that this is the right policy! Nothing is so hateful to a real lover as an easy, accommodating, altruistic affection—thoroughly Christian in sentiment, and with no more shape of its own than a pillow! Romance flies at the mere mention of Christian altruism; and the essence of love is romance.

Hence not only technical obstacles, but essential differences are necessary to the growth of the passion. Differences of age, differences of sex, differences of class, temperament, hereditary strain, learning, accomplishment, and so forth—if not *too* great—are all necessary and valuable. They all mean romance, and contribute to that exchange of essences which we saw was the primitive protozoic law. It is quite probable that the abiding romance between the sexes—so much greater as a rule than that between two of like sex—is due to the fact that the man and the woman never really understand each other; each to the other is a figure in cloudland, sometimes truly divine, sometimes alas! quite the reverse; but never clear and obvious in outline, as a simple mortal may be expected to be.

But to return to the subject of pain and suffering. There is something more in their work than merely to reveal to the lover the extent or the depth of his own love. They have something surely to do with the inner realities of the affair, with the moulding or hammering or welding process whereby union is effected and, in some sense, a new being created. It seems as if when two naked souls approach, or come anywhere near contact with each other, the one inevitably burns or scorches the other. The intense chemistry of the psychic elements produces something like an actual flame. A fresh combination is entered into, profound transformations are effected, strange forces liberated, and a new personality perhaps created; and the accomplishment and evidence of the whole process is by no means only joy, but agony also, even as childbirth is.

All one can reasonably do is to endure. It is no good *making a fuss*. In affairs of the heart what we call suffering corresponds to what we call labor or effort in affairs of the body. When you put your shoulder to the cart-wheel you feel the pain and pressure of the effort, but that assures you that you are exercising a force, that something is being done; so suffering of the heart assures you that something is being done in that other and less tangible world. To scold and scowl and blame your loved one is the stupidest thing you can do. And worse than stupid, it is useless. For it can only alienate. Probably that other one is suffering as well as you—possibly more than you, possibly a good deal less. What does it matter? The suffering is there and must be borne; the work, whatever it is, is being done; the transformation is being effected. Do you want your beloved to suffer instead of you, or simply because you are suffering? Or is it Pity you desire rather than Love.

On the other hand, these things borne in silence have, I believe, an extraordinary effect. They pull people to you by quite invisible cords. As I have said, the fact of heart-strain and tension shows that there is a pressure or pull being exerted somewhere. Though the cord be invisible, there is someone at the other end (though not perhaps quite the one you supposed) who responds.

Words anyhow, in matters of love, are rather foolish; they are worse than foolish, they are useless; and again they are worse than useless, for they are misleading. Love is an art. "It must be revealed by *acts*," says a Swiss writer, "and not *betrayed* by words." And Havelock Ellis, speaking further of the mistake of relying on declarations and asservations, says:[26] "This is scarcely realized by those ill-advised lovers who consider that the first step in courtship—and perhaps even the whole of courtship—is for a man to ask a woman to be his wife. That is so far from being the case that it constantly happens that the premature exhibition of so large a demand at once and forever damns all the wooer's chances." And in another passage he says:[27] "Love's requests cannot be made in words, nor truthfully answered in words: a fine divination is still needed as long as love lasts."

Love is an art. As no mere talk can convey the meaning of a piece of music or a beautiful poem, so no verbal declaration can come anywhere near expressing what the lover wants to say. And for one very good and sufficient reason (among others)—namely, that he does not know himself! Under these circumstances to say anything is almost certainly to say something misleading or false. And the decent lover knows this and holds his tongue. To talk about your devotion is to kill it—moreover, it is to render it banal and suspect in the eyes of your beloved.

Nevertheless though he cannot describe or explain what he wants to say, the lover can *feel* it—is feeling it all the time; and this feeling, like other feelings, he can express by indirections—by symbols, by actions, by the alphabet of deed and gesture, and all the hieroglyphics of Life and Art. Like the animals and the angels and all the blessed creatures who don't *talk*, he can communicate in the ancient, primeval, universal language of all creation, in the language which is itself creation.

CHAPTER IV

ITS ULTIMATE MEANINGS

"To talk about your devotion is to kill it." Perhaps one ought even to say that to talk at all is to kill it! One often thinks what divine and beautiful creatures—men and women—there are all around, how loving and lovable, how gracious in their charm, how grand in their destiny!—if indeed they could only be persuaded to remain within that magic circle of silence. And then alas! one of these divinities begins to talk—and it is like the fair woman in the fable, out of whose mouth, whenever she opened it, there jumped a *mouse*! The shock is almost more than one can bear. Not that the shock proceeds from the ignorance displayed—for the animals and even the angels are deliciously ignorant—but from the revelations which speech unconsciously makes of certain states of the soul—from the strange *falsity* which is too often heard in the words, and in the very tones of the voice.

But Love burns this falsity away. That is why love—even rude and rampant and outrageous love—does more for the moralizing of poor humanity than a hundred thousand Sunday schools. It cleans the little human soul from the clustered lies in which it has nested itself—from the petty conceits and deceits and cowardices and covert meannesses—and all the things that fly from the tip of the tongue directly the mouth opens. It burns and cleans them away, and leaves the lover speechless—but approximately honest!

Love is an art, and the greatest of the Arts—and the truth of it cannot be said in words; that is, in any direct use of words. You may write a sonnet, of course, to your mistress's eyebrow; but that is work, that is doing something; it is or is trying to be, a work of Art—and anyhow your mistress is not obliged to read it! Or you may take a more decisive line to express your feelings—by slaying your rival, for instance, with a sword. That is allowable. But to bore the lady with protestations, and to demand definite replies (that is, to tell lies yourself, and to compel her to tell lies), is both foolish and wicked.

The expression of Love is a great art, and it needs man's highest ingenuity and capacity to become skilled in it—but in the public mind it is an art utterly neglected and despised, and it is only by a very few (and those not always the most 'respectable') that it is really cultivated. It is a great art, for the same reason that the expression of Beauty is a great art—for the reason that Love itself (like Beauty) belongs to another plane of existence than the plane of ordinary life and speech.

Speech is man's great prerogative, which differentiates him from the other creatures, and of which he is, especially during the Civilization period, so proud. The animals do not use it, because they have not arrived at the need of it; the angels do not use it, because they have passed beyond the need. It belongs to the second stage of human consciousness, that which is founded on self-consciousness—on the rooted consciousness of the self as something solitary, apart from others, even antagonistic to them, the centre (strange contradiction in terms!) even among millions of other centres, to which everything has to be referred. The whole of ordinary speech proceeds, and has proceeded, from this kind of self-consciousness—is generated from it, describes it, analyzes it, pictures it forth and expresses it—and in the upshot is just as muddled and illusive and unsatisfactory as the thing it proceeds from. And *Love*, which is *not* founded on that kind of self-consciousness—which is in fact the denial of self-centration—has no use for it. Love can only say what it wants by the language of life, action, song, sacrifice, ravishment, death, and the great panorama of creation.

Self-consciousness is fatal to love. The self-conscious lover never 'arrives.' The woman looks at him—and then she looks at something more interesting. And so too the whole modern period of commercial civilization and Christianity has been fatal to love; for both these great movements have concentrated the thoughts of men on their own individual salvation—Christianity on the salvation of their souls, and commercialism on the salvation of their money-bags. They have bred the self-regarding consciousness in the highest degree; and so—though they may have had their uses and their parts to play in the history of mankind, they have been fatal to the communal spirit in society, and they have been fatal to the glad expression of the soul in private life.

Self-consciousness is fatal to love, which is the true expression of the soul. And it is curious how (for some occult reason) the whole treatment of the subject in our modern world drives it along this painful mirror-lined ravine—how the child is brought up in ignorance and darkness, amid averted faces and frowns, and always the thought of self and its own wickedness is thrust upon it, and never the good and the beauty of the loved one; how the same attitude continues into years of maturity; how somehow self-forgetting heroisms for the sake of love are made difficult in modern life; how even the act of intercourse itself, instead of taking place in the open air—in touch with the great and abounding life of Nature—is generally consummated in closed and stuffy rooms, the symbols of mental darkness and morbidity, and the breeding-ground of the pettier elements of human nature.[28]

We have said that for any lasting alliance, or really big and satisfactory love-affair, plenty of *time* should be given. Perhaps it is a good rule (if any rule in such matters can be good) never to act until one is practically compelled by one's feelings to do so. At any rate, the opposite policy—that of letting off steam, or giving expression to one's sentiments, at the slightest pressure—is an obvious mistake. It gives no chance for the depths to be stirred, or the big forces to come into play. Some degree, too, of self-repression and holding back on the part of the man gives time, as we have said, for the woman's love-feelings to unfold and define themselves. But there is a limit here, and even sympathy and consideration are not always in place with love. There is something bigger—titanic, elemental—which must also have its way. And, after all, Force (if only appropriately used) is the greatest of compliments. I think every woman, in her heart of hearts, *wishes* to be ravished; but naturally it must be by the right man. This is the compliment which is the most grateful of all to receive, because it is most sincere; and this is the compliment which is the most difficult of all to pay—because nothing but the finest instinct can decide when it is appropriate; and if by chance it is inappropriate the cause is *ipso facto* ruined.

Nature prizes strength and power; and so likewise does love, which moves in the heart of Nature and shares her secrets. To regard Love as a kind of refined and delicate altruism is, as we have already hinted, drivelling nonsense. To the lover in general violence is more endurable than indifference; and many lovers are of such temperament that blows and kicks (actual or metaphorical) stimulate and increase their ardor. Even Ovid—who must have been something of a gay dog in his day—says,"*non nisi læsus amo*." There is a feeling that at all costs one must come to close quarters with the beloved—if not in the mimic battles of sex, then in quite serious and hostile encounters. To reach the other one somehow, to leave one's mark, one's impress on the beloved—or *vice versa* to *be* reached and to *feel* the impress—is a necessity. I sometimes think that this is the explanation of those strange cases in which a man, mad with love, and unable to satisfy his passion, *kills* the girl he loves. I don't think it is hypothetical jealousy of a possible other lover. I think it is something much more direct than that—the blind urge to reach her very actual self, even if it be only with knife or bullet. I am sure that this is the explanation of those many cases of unhappily married folk who everlastingly nag at each other, and yet will not on any account part company. They cannot love each other properly, and yet they cannot leave each other alone. A strange madness urges them into continual contact and collision.

But yet possibly there is even something more in the whole thing, on and beyond what is here indicated. In the extraordinary and often agonizing experiences attending the matter of 'falling in love,' great changes, as we have already suggested, are being wrought in the human being. Astounding inner convulsions and conversions take place—rejections of old habits, adoptions of new ones. The presence of the beloved exercises this magical selective and reconstructive influence—and that independently to a large degree of whether the relation is a happy and 'successful' one, or whether it is contrary and unsuccessful. The main thing is contact, and the coming of one person into touch with the other.

We have seen, in the case of the Protozoa, the amazing fact of the 'maturation-divisions' and the 'extrusion of polar bodies' as a preparation for conjugation—how, when the two cells which are about to unite approach each other, changes take place already before they come into contact, and half the chromatin elements from one cell are expelled, and half the chromatin elements also from the other. What the exact nature of this division and extrusion may be is a thing not yet known, but there seems every reason to believe that it is of such a character as to leave the residual elements on both sides complementary to one another—so that when united they shall restore the total attributes of the race-life, only perhaps in a new and unprecedented combination. The Protozoa in fact 'prepare' themselves for conjugation and realization of the race-life, by casting out certain elements which would interfere with this realization. And we may well ask ourselves whether in the case of Man the convulsions and conversions of which we have spoken have not the same purpose and result, or something much resembling it. Whatever really takes place in the unseen world in the case of human Love, we cannot but be persuaded that it is something of very far-reaching and long-lasting import; and to find that the process should often involve great pain to the little mortals concerned seems readily conceivable and by no means unnatural.

The complementary nature of love is a thing which has often been pointed out—how the dark marries the fair, the tall the short, the active the lethargic, and so forth. Schopenhauer, in his *Welt als Wille und Vorstellung*, has made a special study of this subject. Plato, Darwin, and others have alluded to it. It seems as if, in Love, the creature—to use Dante Rossetti's expression—feels a "poignant thirst and exquisite hunger" for that other one who will supply the elements wanting in himself, who will restore the balance, and fill up the round of the race ideal. And as every one of us is eccentric and out of balance and perfection on one side or another, so it almost seems as if for every one there must be, on the other side, a complementary character to be found—who needs *something* at any rate of what we can supply. And this consideration may yield us the motto—however painfully conscious we may be of our own weaknesses and deficiencies and follies and vices and general ungainliness—the motto of "Never despair!" Innocent folk, whose studies of this subject have been chiefly perhaps derived from penny novelettes—are sometimes inclined to think that love is a stereotyped affair occurring in a certain pattern and under certain conditions between the ages of 18 and 35; and that if you are not between these ages and are not fortunate enough to have a good complexion and a nicely formed aquiline nose, you may as well abandon hope! They suppose that there is a certain thing called a Man, and another certain thing called a Woman, and that the combination of these two forms a third quite stereotyped thing called Marriage, *and there is an end of it.*

But by some kind of Providential arrangement it appears that the actual facts are very different—that there are really hundreds of thousands of different kinds of men, and hundreds of thousands of different kinds of women, and consequently thousands of millions of different kinds of marriage; that there are no limits of grace or comeliness, or of character and accomplishment, or even of infirmity or age, within which love is obliged to move; and that there is no defect, of body or mind, which is of necessity a bar—which may not even (to some special other person) become an object of attraction. Thus it is that the ugly and deformed have no great difficulty in finding their mates—as a visit to the seaside on a bank-holiday speedily convinces us; a squint may be a positive attraction to some, as it is said to have been to the philosopher Descartes, and marks of smallpox indispensable to others;[29] while I have read of a case somewhere, where the man was immediately stirred to romance by the sight of a wooden leg in a woman![30]

But apart from these extreme instances which may be due to special causes, the general principle of compensation through opposites is very obvious and marked. The fluffy and absurd little woman is selected by a tall and statuesque grenadier; the tall and statuesque lady is made love to by a man who has to stand on a chair to kiss her; the society elegant takes to a snuffy and preposterous professor; the bookish scholar (as in *Jude the Obscure*) to a mere whore; the clever beauty (as in *L'homme qui rit*) to a grinning clown; and of course the 'wicked' man is always saved by the saintly woman. The masculine, virago-like woman, on the other hand, finds a man who positively *likes* being beaten with a stick; and the miaowling, aimlessly amiable female gets a bully for a husband (and one can only say, "Serve them both right")... Finally, the well-formed aquiline nose insists on marrying a pug nose—and this apparently quite regardless of what the other bodily and mental parts may be, or what they may want.

Everyone knows cases of quite young men who only love women of really advanced age, beyond the limit of childbirth; and these are curious because they seem to point to impelling forces in love beyond and independent of generation and race-perpetuation, and therefore lying outside of the Schopenhauerian explanations. And similarly we all know cases of young girls who are deadly earnest in their affection for quite old men, men who might well be their fathers or grandfathers, but hardly, one would think, their husbands. In these cases it looks as if the young thing needs and seeks a parent as well as a lover—the two in one, combined. And where such love is returned, it is returned in a kind of protective love, rather than an amative love—or at any rate as a love in which the protective and amative characters are closely united.

Similarly there are numbers of cases in which mature or quite grown men and women only love (passionately and devotedly) boys and girls of immature age—their love for them ceasing from its ardor and intensity when the objects of devotion reach the age, say, of twenty or twenty-one. And in many of these cases the love is ardently returned. Here, again, it is evidently not a case of generation or race-perpetuation, but simply of compensation—the young thing requiring the help and protection of the older, and the older requiring an outlet for the protective instinct—a case of exchange of essences and qualities which (if at all decently and sensibly managed) might well go to the building up of a full and well-rounded life on either side.

In all these cases (and the above are of course only samples out of thousands) we seem to see an effort of the race-life to restore its total quality—to restore it through the operation of love—either by completing and rounding out the life of the individuals concerned, or by uniting some of their characteristics in the progeny. I say 'seem to see,' because we cannot well suppose that this gives a *complete* account of the matter, or that it explains the whole meaning of Love; but it at any rate suggests an important aspect of the question. The full quality of the race-life is always building itself up and restoring itself in this manner. A process of Regeneration is always going on. And this process, as suggested before, is more fundamental even than Generation—or it is a process of which Generation is only one department.

Regeneration is the key to the meaning of love—to be in the first place born again *in* some one else or *through* some one else; in the second place only, to be born again through a child. As in the Protozoa, so among human beings, generation alone can hardly be looked upon as the primary object of conjugation; for, among the latter, out of myriads of unions vast numbers are as a matter of fact infertile, and a considerable percentage (as indicated above) are quite *necessarily* infertile, and yet these infertile unions are quite as close, and the love concerned in them quite as intense and penetrating, as in the case of the fertile ones. "If a girl were free to choose according to her inclinations," says Florence Farr in an eloquent plea for the economic independence of women,[31] "there is practically no doubt that she would choose the right father for her child, however badly she might choose a life-long companion for herself." In this passage the authoress seems to suggest (perhaps following Schopenhauer) that the generation of a perfect child is the one main even though unconscious purpose of love-union, and that the individual parent-lives may instinctively be sacrificed for this object. And there no doubt is so far truth in this, that the tremendous forces of love often pay little respect to the world conveniences and compatibilities of the lovers themselves, and that often (as indeed also among the Protozoa) the parent's life is rudely and ruthlessly sacrificed for the birth of the next generation. Still, even so, I think the statement as put here is risky, both as a matter of fact and as a matter of theory. Would it not be more correct or less risky to say: "If a girl were free to choose, she would choose the man who most completely compensated and rounded out her own qualities, physical and mental (and *so* would be likely to get her a fine babe), even though he might not prove the best of companions?"

It is curious, as we have suggested before, how married folk often quarrel to desperation on the surface, and yet seem to have a deep and permanent hold on each other—returning together again even after separation. It seems in these cases as if they mutually obtained a stimulus from each other, even by their strife, which they could not get elsewhere. *Iræ amantium redintegratio amoris.* The idea, too, that the great and primal object of union is to be sought in *the next generation* has something unsatisfactory about it. Why not in *this* generation? Why should the blessedness of mankind always be deferred to posterity? It is not merely, I take it, the *perpetuation* of the race which is the purpose of love, but the perfection of the race, the completeness and adequacy of its self-expression, which love may make possible to-day just as well as to-morrow. Ellen Key, in that fine book, *Liebe und Ehe*,[32] expresses this well when she says: "Love seeks union, not only in connection with the creation of a new being, but also because two beings *through one another* may become a new being, and a greater than either could be of itself alone."

The complementary nature of sex-attraction was made much of by that youthful genius Otto Weininger, who in his book, *Sex and Character*,[33] has a chapter on the laws of Sexual Attractions in which, in the true German manner, he not only gives an algebraic formula for the different types of men and women, but a formula also for the force of attraction between any two given individuals—which latter of course becomes infinite when the two individuals are exactly complementary to each other! Dr. Magnus Hirschfeld, in his very interesting work, *Die Transvestiten*,[34] goes even more into detail than does Weininger on the subject of the variations of human type in special regard to sex-characteristics. Sex-characteristics, he explains, may be divided into four groups, of which two are physiological, namely the primary characteristics (the sex organs and adjuncts) and the secondary (the hair, the voice, the breasts, and so forth); and two are psychological or related (like love-sentiment, mental habit, dress, and so forth). Each of the four groups includes about four different elements; so that altogether he tabulates sixteen elements in the human being—each of which may vary independently of the other fifteen, and take on at least three possible forms, either distinctly masculine, distinctly feminine, or intermediate. Calculating up the number of different types which these variations would thus give rise to, he arrives at the figure 43,,!—which figure, I think we may say, we need not analyze further, since it is certainly quite large enough for all practical purposes! And really though we may mock a little at these fanciful divisions and dissections of human nature, they do help us to realize the enormous, the astounding number of varieties of which it is susceptible. And if again we consider that among the supposed forty-three millions each variety would have its counter type or complementary individual, then we realize the enormous number of perfect unions which would be theoretically possible, and the enormous number of distinct and different ways in which the race-life could thus find adequate and admirable expression for itself.

However, we are here getting into a somewhat abstract region. To return to the practical, the complementary idea certainly seems to account for much of human union; for though there are but few cases in which the qualities of the uniting parties are really quite complementary to each other, yet it is obvious that each person tends to seek and admire attributes in the other which he himself possesses only in small degree. At the same time, it must not be forgotten that *some* common qualities and common ground are necessary as a basis for affection, and that sympathy and agreement in like interests and habits are at least as powerful a bond as admiration of opposites. It sometimes happens that there are immense romances between people of quite different classes and habits of life, or of quite different race and color; and they see, for the moment, flaming ideals and wonder-worlds in each other. But unions in such cases are doubtful and dangerous, because so often the common ground of sympathy and mutual understanding will be too limited; and hereditary instincts and influences, deep-lying and deep-working, will call the wanderers away, even from the star which they seek to follow.

Sympathy with and understanding of the person one lives with must be cultivated to the last degree possible, because it is a condition of any real and permanent alliance. And it may even go so far (and should go so far) as a frank understanding and tolerance of such person's *other* loves. After all, it seldom happens, with any one who has more than one or two great interests in life, that he finds a mate who can sympathize with or understand them all. In that case a certain portion of his personality is left out in the cold, as it were; and if this is an important portion it seems perfectly natural for him to seek for a mate or a lover on that side too. Two such loves are often perfectly compatible and reconcilable—though naturally one will be the dominant love, and the other subsidiary, and if such secondary loves are good-humoredly tolerated and admitted, the effect will generally be to confirm the first and original alliance all the more.

All this, however, does not mean that a man can well be 'in love' with two women, for instance, at the same time. To love is a very different thing from being 'in love'; and the latter indicates a torrent-rush of feeling which necessarily can only move towards one person at a time. (A standing flood of water may embrace and surround several islands, but it cannot very well *flow* in more than one direction at once.) But this torrent-rush does not last forever, and in due time it subsides into the quiescent and lake-like stage—unless indeed it runs itself out and disappears altogether.

Against this running out and disappearance it is part of the Art of Love to be able to guard. It has sometimes been argued that familiarity is of necessity fatal; and that it is useless to contend against this sinister tendency implanted in the very nature of love itself. But this contention contains only a very partial truth. It is true that in physical love there is a certain physical polarity which, like electric polarity, tends to equate itself by contact. The exchange of essences—which we saw as a chief phenomenon of conjugation, from the protozoa upwards—completes itself in any given case after a given time; and after that becomes comparatively quiescent. The same with the exchange of mental essences. Two people, after years, cease to exchange their views and opinions with the same vitality as at first; they lose their snap and crackle with regard to each other—and naturally, because they now know each other's minds perfectly, and have perhaps modified them mutually to the point of likeness. But this only means, or should mean in a healthy case, that their interest in each other has passed into another plane, that the *venue* of Love has been removed to another court. If something has been lost in respect of the physical rush and torrent, and something in respect of the mental breeze and sparkle, great things have been gained in the ever-widening assurance and confidence of spiritual unity, and a kind of lake-like calm which indeed reflects the heavens. And under all, still in the depths, one may be conscious of a subtle flow and interchange, yet going on between the two personalities and relating itself to some deep and unseen movements far down in the heart of Nature.

Of course for this continuance and permanence of love there must be a certain amount of continence, not only physical, but on the emotional plane as well. Anything like nausea, created by excess on either of these planes, has to be avoided. New subjects of interest, and points of contact, must be sought; temporary absences rather encouraged than deprecated; and lesser loves, as we have already hinted, not turned into gages of battle. Few things, in fact, endear one to a partner so much as the sense that one can freely confide to him or her one's *affaires de cœur*, and when a man and wife have reached this point of confidence in their relation to each other, it may fairly then be said (however shocking this may sound to the orthodox) that their union is permanent and assured.

Nothing can, in the longer enduring values of love, well take the place of some such chivalrous mutual consideration which reaches the finest fibres of the heart, and offers a perfect freedom even there. Ellen Key—to quote her *Ueber Liebe und Ehe*[35] again—says, "Fidelity [in love] can never be promised, but may be *won afresh* every day;" and she continues, "It is sad that this truth—which was clear enough to the chivalrous sentiment of the old courts of Love—must still to-day be insisted on. One of the reasons, in fact, which these courts gave, why love was not compatible with Marriage, was 'that the wife could never expect from her husband the fine consideration that the Lover is bound to exhibit, because the latter only receives as a favor what the husband takes as his right.'" To preserve love through years and years with this halo of romance still about it, and this tenderness of devotion which means a daily renewed gift of freedom, is indeed a great Art. It is a great and difficult Art, but one which is assuredly "worth while."

The passion altogether, and in all its aspects, is a wonderful thing; and perhaps, as remarked before, the less said about it, the better! When people—I would say—come (not without clatter) and offer you their hearts, do not pay *too* much attention. What they offer may be genuine, or it may not—they themselves probably do not know. Nor do *you* also fall into a like mistake, offering something which you have not the power to give—or to withhold. Silence and Time alone avail. These things lie on the knees of the gods; which place—though it may seem, as someone has said, 'rather cold and uncomfortable'—is perhaps the best place for them.

CHAPTER V

THE ART OF DYING

WE have suggested in the last paper that some day possibly we may arrive at an intelligent handling of love and its problems, by which at length the passion may cease to be the cause of endless shipwreck and despair to mortals, and become a favorable and friendly divinity obedient to our service. Somewhat thus has been man's experience with all the great powers of Nature—with fire and flood on the earth, with the winds and lightning of heaven. With intelligent treatment they have become his very ready helpers and allies. And, as indicated in the outset of this book, we may fairly expect the same conclusion with regard to the great natural event and process termed Death. The time has come when we are really called upon to face up to the fact of our decease from the present conditions of life, physical and mental; when we are called upon to study and to understand this fact, and by understanding to become masters of the change which it represents—and able to convert it to our great use and advantage.

Hitherto—as I shall have occasion presently to point out—there has been singularly little study of this science, either from the clinical, the physiological, or the psychological points of view; and the art of dying, for example (which is the subject of this chapter), seems to have been entirely neglected.

No doubt it may be said that this is a difficult art—difficult to study, and more difficult still to practise; yet, after all, that seems only the more reason for approaching it. The art of *avoiding* death commands much attention, and there are hundreds and thousands of books on that subject; yet since none can really avoid the experience and all must sooner or later pass through it, it might be thought that the art of meeting one's end with discretion and presence of mind would at least command as much attention.

There ought, one would say—and considering the continual presence of this great ocean waiting to receive us—to be lessons on the subject of its navigation free of charge, and available for all who wish, just as there are lessons in swimming for sailors. And though it may be true that since, as a rule, one cannot die more than once, it is difficult to obtain the needed practice, yet even so one may with perseverance get some approach to doing so. There are a good many recorded cases of people who have apparently died, and after an interval of a few minutes or a few hours have come to life again. I knew a married lady, some years back, who after a long period of illness was given up by the doctors, and gradually sank till to all appearances she passed away. The medical man pronounced life to be extinct, and the relatives began to make the usual arrangements for her funeral. However, being devoted to her children, and anxious to see them through a critical period, she had made up her mind *not* to die, and being a woman of strong will she clung to her resolution. Two or three hours elapsed, and then, to the surprise and joy of her friends she returned from 'the other side'—after which she lived three or four years, sufficiently long to carry out what was needed for her family. And though in this case she had no very distinct experience to report of another state of existence, yet the fact of her 'will to live' having persevered through the sleep or apparent death of her body and upper mind, was sufficient to convince her of survival of some sort on a deeper plane, and to disarm all fear and hesitation when death finally came.

Probably, on the ordinary mental plane, death very much resembles sleep, and its actual arrival is almost imperceptible; but, in the deeper regions of the mind, there are not unfrequently signs or suggestions of a great awakening. An expression of ecstasy often overspreads the features; sometimes there are sudden apparent recognitions of friends who have already passed away;[36] in many cases there seems to be a great extension of memory and perception; and in not a few a distinct sensation of flying or moving upwards.[37] To these and other similar considerations I shall return later. At present I would prefer to keep to the more physical aspects of the question; but even so far, one cannot help feeling that—whatever collateral drawbacks there may be in death—in the way of painful illness, parting with friends, disturbance and abandonment of plans, and so forth—the experience itself must be enormously interesting. Talk about starting on a journey; but what must the longest sea-voyage be, compared with this one, with its wonderful vista, and visions, and voices calling? And again, since it is an experience that all must go through, and that countless millons of our fellows *have* gone through and are still continually going through, for that very reason alone it has a fascination; and one feels that had one the opportunity to avoid it one would hardly wish to do so.

As I have said, it is curious that there is next to no instruction or guidance commonly provided or accessible in this matter. I mean especially on the physical side. What are our medical folk doing? There are lots of books on childbirth and the science of parturition, and the best methods of making the transition easy; but when it comes to the end of life and the event corresponding and complementary to birth, there is little except silence and dismay.

The usual course of preparation for this most important event seems to be (barring accidents) something as follows:—a physically unhealthy and morally stupid life, which inevitably leads to degenerative tendencies and ultimately to distinct disease; then one or two breakdowns, which lead to panic, and the summoning of doctors; then partial recovery, and a repetition *da capo* of the whole series, without any of the least improvement in the general style of life; then of course worse breakdown and panic, leading at last to violent drugs, injections, operations, and so forth, in the hope of prolonging existence a few hours; and finally death arriving, not graciously, but in the sense of a dismal defeat and rout to everybody concerned; and to the patient a hurried, confused and embittered end, robbed of all decency and dignity.

Now this won't do! When one thinks of the deaths of animals—so composed on the whole—the calm, the quietude, the dignity even, and the absence as a rule of very acute or obvious suffering; or when one thinks of the very similar conditions of death among many savage peoples; one cannot but ask, Why this difference? One cannot but say, It really *will not do* for us 'the heirs of all the ages' to go on behaving in this feeble and foolish way—leading lives which utterly unfit us for the inevitable end of life, and stricken with most incompetent panic and dismay when the very thing arrives which we have foreseen and which we have had such ample time to prepare for.

Death—from whatever point of view we look at it—seems to be a break-up of the unity of the creature.[38] It is a dislocation and to some degree a rending asunder. But such dislocation and break-up may be of a healthy and normal type, or it may be unhealthy and of the nature of disease. In the first case it may chiefly consist in the getting rid or shedding off of an out-worn husk, which is simply left behind—much in the same way as the chrysalis sheath of a moth or other insect is left behind, or as the husks of a growing bud or bulb are peeled off. Many an old person seems to die in this way—the body being the scene of little or no disturbance or conflict, but simply withering up, while often at the same time the spiritual nature of the man becomes strangely luminous and penetrating. Here there is a certain dislocation, but no painful rending asunder. The centre of life seems merely to retire to a more inward and subtle region, where it perchance nourishes an even brighter flame than before; and the outer body is peeled off as a sort of outworn shell. But in other cases death is undoubtedly very different. Instead of the one centre simply withdrawing inward in the way indicated, while at the same time preserving almost to the last a general unity of the creature, rebellious and insubordinate centres spring up and introduce serious conflict into the organism. These are of course diseases, or centres of disease—either in the body, like tumors, alien growths, nests of microbes, and so forth; or in the mind, like violent passions, greeds, anxieties, fears, rigid habits. And forming thus independent centres they tear and rend the body and mind between them till at last death supervenes—not at all on account of the voluntary withdrawal of the inner person to more ethereal regions, but simply through the destruction of the organism in which that person functions.

It is evident (whatever view one may take of that inner person and its perduration into other regions of existence) that the former mode of death is the more normal, natural and desirable of the two, and the one which we should encourage and cultivate; and that the latter is likely to be painful, undignified, and even repulsive.

From this point of view, to strengthen the organizing, regulating power of the body, as against local growths and insurgencies, seems (in general terms) the best line to take—the best way of prolonging life, and of rendering death fairly easy and negotiable. The outlying centres—as represented by the various organs and faculties, both of the body and of the mind—have to be kept during life in subordination to the main centre, and as far as possible in decent harness and exercise, so as to become neither too slack on the one hand, nor too rowdy and insolent on the other. In this way, when the vital forces decay, these organs and faculties remain still subservient to the central being, and becoming comparatively quiescent make room for its further passage and development. There are, indeed, some cases of death, in which the whole inner spirit and consciousness of the man seems to pass on unchanged, while the rabble rout of the body simply falls away, or is left behind, like a disused garment or husk as we have said.

It should, however, be noted that the strengthening of the organizing and regulating forces does not and must not mean the introduction of rigid and quasi-tyrannical habits (however 'good' such habits may be supposed to be). The interior Person—as we shall see later—is far too great and free to be adequately represented by any such habits or regulations, even the 'best,' and they really belong to the lower mind or body. Their dominance leads to an ossifying or woodening and valetudinarian tendency in the organism, which is as bad in its way as the uncontrolled or inflammatory tendency.

To avoid these opposite pitfalls, and to live sanely and sensibly, in a certain close touch with Nature and with the roots of human life, is no doubt difficult, especially under the ordinary conditions of civilization; yet it is surely well worth while—both for the sake of life itself and for the termination of it. And to keep a certain command of the situation during the mid-period of one's day is probably the best way toward commanding the situation at the end. But the ordinary medical methods—with their drugs, their stimulants, their sleeping-draughts, their operations, their injections of morphia, serums, and so forth, are surely acting all the time in the opposite direction. Their tendency surely is to confuse and weaken the central agency, while at the same time they excite and sometimes madden the local centres—till not unfrequently the patient dies, confused, unconscious, wrecked, and a mass of disorders and corruption. The launching of a ship on the great ocean is a thing that is prepared for, even during all the period when the vessel is being built and perfected. I am not a professional; but will no one write a manual on the subject, even from the medical and physiological point of view—How to prepare for death.... How to go through this great change with some degree of satisfaction, command, and intelligence? Above all, may we have a truce to the so common and unworthy conspiracies between doctors, nurses, and relatives, by which for the sake of keeping the patient a few hours (or at most a few days) longer alive, the unfortunate one—instead of being let alone and allowed to die peacefully as far as may be, and as indeed in nine cases out of ten he himself desires—is on the contrary tormented (defenceless as he is) with operations, inoculations and medical insults of all kinds up to the very last? The thing has become a positive scandal; and though the ignorant importunities of lay relatives may sometimes be deplorable, yet the prospect in one's last moments of falling into the hands of professionals is even worse, and adds a new terror to dissolution. It is at any rate a consolation to know that whatever pains and torments of illness may have preceded, they generally pass away before the end; and notwithstanding such current expressions as 'death-agonies,' 'last struggle,' and so forth, the hour of death itself is mercifully calm and peaceful. Walt Whitman, who, in his hospital labors in the American Civil War, must have been present at a vast number of deathbeds, has recorded that in the great majority of cases the end comes quite simply, as an ordinary event of the day, "like having your breakfast." "Death is no more painful than birth," says Dr. Edward Clark in his book on *Visions: a Study of False Sight*;[39] and most doctors will agree to the general truth of this expression.

There is a certain sacredness in Death, which should surely be respected. There is too, we may say, in most cases, a sure instinct which comes to the patient of what is impending and of what is needed; and every effort should be made to secure to the sufferer a quiet period during which he may effect the passage, for himself, disturbed as little as possible by the grief of friends or the interferences of attendants.

II. PSYCHICAL

We may now discuss the subject in hand somewhat more from the psychical side. Not that in these matters the physical and the psychical can ever be completely dissociated, but that having in the preceding section leaned more to the physical side it may be convenient now to lean rather to the psychical.

And there is certainly an advantage here—namely, that from this side we may not unreasonably say that the art of dying *can* be practised: it is really possible to approach or even perhaps to pass through Death on the mental plane, by voluntary effort. Most people regard the loss of ordinary consciousness (apart from sleep) with something like terror and horror. The best way to dispel that fear is to walk through the gate oneself every day—to divest oneself of that consciousness, and, mentally speaking, to die from time to time. Then one may get accustomed to it.

Of all the hard facts of Science: as that fire will burn, that water will freeze, that the earth spins on its axis, and so forth, I know of none more solid and fundamental than the fact that if you inhibit thought (and persevere) you come at length to a region of consciousness below or behind thought, and different from ordinary thought in its nature and character—a consciousness of quasi-universal quality, and a realization of an altogether vaster self than that to which we are accustomed. And since the ordinary consciousness, with which we are concerned in ordinary life, is before all things founded on the little local self, and is in fact *self*-consciousness in the little local sense, it follows that to pass out of that is to die to the ordinary self and the ordinary world.

It is to die in the ordinary sense, but in another sense it is to wake up and find that the 'I,' one's real, most intimate self, pervades the universe and all other beings—that the mountains and the sea and the stars are a part of one's body and that one's soul is in touch with the souls of all creatures. Yes, far closer than before. It is to be assured of an indestructible immortal life and of a joy immense and inexpressible—"to drink of the deep well of rest and joy, and sit with all the Gods in Paradise."

So great, so splendid is this experience, that it may be said that all minor questions and doubts fall away in face of it; and certain it is that in thousands and thousands of cases the fact of its having come even once to a man has completely revolutionized his subsequent life and outlook on the world.

Of exactly how this inhibition of Thought may be practised, and of all its collateral results and implications it would be out of place to speak now.[40] Sufficient at present to say that with the completion of this inhibition, and the realization of the consequent change of consciousness—even if it be only for a time—the ordinary mental self, with all its worries, cares, limitations, imperfections, and so forth, falls completely off, and lies (for the time) like a thing dead; while the real man practically passes onward into another state of being.

To experience all this with any degree of fulness, is to know that you have passed through Death; because whatever destruction physical death may bring to your local senses and faculties, you know that it will not affect that deeper Self. I mean that having already become aware of your real self as pervading the life of other creatures, and moving in other bodies than your so-called own, it clearly does not so very much matter whether the one body remains or passes. It may make a difference certainly, but not a fatal or insuperable difference. The vast ocean of the consciousness into which you have been admitted will not be profoundly affected, even by the abstraction of a pearl-shell from its shore.

We have spoken of the Protozoa more than once in these connections; and it has been said that the Protozoa have been considered immortal because, though they divide into separate cells or organisms, the life remains continuous; and because though some of the descendant cells may die yet the life goes on—so that even in the hundredth generation the self or ego of a particular cell may be identical with that of the first parent. And in the case we are considering we have something similar, for when the common life of souls is once recognized and experienced, it is clear that nothing can destroy it. It simply passes from one form to another. And we may perhaps say that as the Protozoa attain to a kind of immortality *below* death, or prior to its appearance in the world, so the emancipated or freed soul attains to immortality above and beyond death—passing *over* death, in fact, as a mere detail in its career.

I say, this heart and kernel of a great and immortal self, this consciousness of a powerful and continuing life within, *is* there—however deeply it may be buried—within each person; and its discovery is open to everyone who will truly and persistently seek for it. And I say that I regard the discovery of this experience—with its accompanying sense of rest, content, expansion, power, joy, and even omniscience and immensity—as the most fundamental and important fact hitherto of human knowledge and scientific inquiry, and one verified and corroborated by thousands and even millions of human kind. Doubtless, as already suggested, questions may arise and will arise as to the exact nature of this continuing life, its exact relation to the local personal consciousness, as well as to what is called the sublimal self—how far definite personality and memory go with it, and so forth. These questions we may return to later. At present let us simply rest on the experience itself.

When Death is at hand, or its oncoming cannot long be delayed, there is still *that* to remember, to revert to, to cling to. And the more often we have made the experience our very own, in life, the easier will it be to hold on to at the close. Whatever physical death may bring—in the way of pain or distress or dislocation of faculty—there still remains that indefeasible fact, the certainty of the survival of the deepest, most universal portion of our natures. In some cases this deepest consciousness does itself remain so clear, so strong that—even through all the obscurations of illness and bodily weakness—death practically brings no break; the body is shed off, more or less like a husk or chrysalis (with effort and struggle perhaps, but without anguish and despair); and the human being passes on to realize under some other form the divine life which he has already partially entered into. I think it evident that this is the state of affairs which we ought to put before ourselves as the goal of our endeavor. It would seem the only condition which secures a sense of continuity in death, or which does not carry with it some threat of failure or extinction. And it suggests to us that our persistent and unremitted effort during ordinary life should be to realize and lay hold of this immortal Thing, to conquer and make our own this very Heart of the universe. It suggests that every magnanimous deed, every self-forgetting enthusiasm, every great and passionate love, every determined effort to get down into the heart and truth of things and below the conventional crust, does really bring us nearer to that attainment, and hasten the day when mankind at large shall indeed finally obtain the victory; and the passage into and through death shall appear natural and simple and clear of obstruction, and even in its due time desirable.

It is clear, however, that in a great number of cases this deepest consciousness, even if it has occasionally during life been reached by the person concerned, has not been sufficiently firmly established to endure through times of sickness, bodily weakness, and mental decay; while again, perhaps in the vast majority of cases, the previous realizations have been almost *nil*, or at most have been too few or too slight to count for much. What are we to say in such cases as these? Even if with the eye of faith or philosophy the bystander may seem to see the immortal spark shining, what consolation or assistance is that to the sufferer himself, who does not perceive or feel it? What is likely to be his experience of dissolution? and what may he fairly expect or look to as any sort of solution of the obscure problem?

To get any kind of answer to these questions and any clear idea of what really happens in the great majority of cases—when the break-up which we call dissolution arrives—it will be necessary to analyze roughly the nature of

Man. We shall then see what are the various elements of that nature, and what their probable destination, respectively. And for the purpose in hand I think we may divide the complete human being into four sections—though remembering of course that the classification proposed, or any such classification, can only be very rough and tentative—namely, into (1) the eternal and immortal Self, of which we have already spoken; (2) the inner personal ego or human soul; (3) the outer personality or animal self; and (4) the actual body. Of these, (1), the eternal Self, is the germ or root of the whole human being; and I think we may even say that all the sections and elements of our human nature are really manifestations or outgrowths from this root (though of course in most cases unconscious of their real belonging or their real source). Then (2), the inner personal self or human soul, includes the finer and subtler elements of 'character'—which we know so well in our friends, yet find so difficult to describe, but which are roughly denoted by such words as affection, courage, wit, sympathy, love of beauty, sense of equality, freedom, self-reliance, determination, and so forth; while (3), the outer personality or animal soul (not at all of course to be despised), is concerned with the more terrestrial desires and passions like pride, ambition, love of possession, jealousy, and especially those that relate themselves directly to the body, *e.g.* desires of food, drink, sex, ease, sleep, and so forth; and finally, (4), the body, includes all the material organs and parts. Other and intermediate subdivisions may be and sometimes are made, but these four will probably suffice for the present—remembering, as already said, that they have only a rough value: hard and fast lines and divisions in such matters being impossible, and the nature of man being really continuous and not built in sections; remembering, too, with regard to all four divisions, that the elements of them are not at all times present in consciousness, but to a large degree remain conscious or hidden or subliminal.

CHAPTER IV

THE PASSAGE OF DEATH

ALLOWING, then, that our human nature may be roughly divided as above into four main constituents, the destiny of two of these at death seems pretty clear. It is clear that (1) the central self remains (whether "we" know it or not) the same as it ever was, and ever will be, eternal, shining in glory and irradiating the world. It goes on, to be the birth-source, may be, of numberless lives to come. On the other hand, it is equally clear that (4) the actual visible tangible body dies, perishes, and is broken up. Though it may return, in its elements and through what we call Nature, into the great birth-source, it ceases as an individual body to exist, and passes even before the eyes of onlookers into other forms. The fate of these two portions of the human entity can hardly be doubted—of the innermost central portion, continuance, with but slow or secular change, if any; of the outermost material shell, immediate decay and dissolution.

What, then, may we suppose is the destiny of the other two portions, the human and the animal part? I think we may fairly suppose that they each share to a considerable degree the destiny of that extreme to which they are closest related. The outer personality or animal life, (3), is most closely related to the body. Its passions and desires (though in themselves psychical and mental entities) look always to the body for their expression and satisfaction. It is difficult to suppose them functioning *without* the body. We cannot, for instance, very well imagine the passion for drink without some kind of mouth or gullet through which to work (though of course it may carry on a sort of dream-activity by representing these channels to itself, or creating mental images of them). And similarly of the passion of personal vanity, or the passion of sex: they refer themselves always to the body, in some degree or other.

It is clear then, I think, that when the body in death breaks up, these psychic elements which function through it and correspond to the various parts and organs—these passions and desires, and with them the whole animal being—are to some extent involved in the ruin. They are (in most cases) smitten with dire suffering and confusion. A terrible misgiving and dismay assault them; and with the break-up and disruption of the body they too experience the agonies of disruption, and foresee their own dissolution and death.[41]

Yet to conclude from this that these elements do absolutely perish, would, I think, be a mistake. For these passional entities and this animal soul, though they seek the body and manifest themselves through it, are not the same as the body. They have a creative power within them.[42] The drunkard, as suggested, deprived of his liquor, represents furiously to himself in imagination the act of drinking: he dreams a gullet a yard long and an endless swallow—and in doing so he actually moulds and modifies his swallowing apparatus. The vain man and the sexual similarly mould and modify their bodies; they contribute to the building of the shapes which they use. And this sort of process going on through the ages has *created* the forms of the animals and mankind, and their respective members and organs.[43] All these things are the expression and manifestation and output of the psychical entities and passions and qualities underlying—which themselves are implicit in the world-soul, which indeed have grown up and manifested themselves out of the world-soul, and which still deeply though hiddenly root back into it.

The most reasonable and obvious answer, then, to the question, What becomes of the animal life and its satellite passions when the body dies? seems to be that under normal conditions they die too—in the sense that they cease to be manifest. They die, like the body, only with this difference, that *being* psychical—*i.e.* having a consciousness and a self underlying, while the body dies back into earth and air, they die back into the psychic roots from which they originally sprang—that is, into that form of the Self or World-soul of which they are the manifestation—as, for instance, in the case of the animals, into the self or soul of the race; in the case of undeveloped man, partly into the soul of the race and partly into the human soul which is affiliated to the soul of the race; and in the case of perfected man, entirely into the human soul or inner personality which, having now found and established its union with the supreme and eternal Self, is no longer dependent on the soul of the race, but has entered into a divine and immortal life of its own.

Thus in entirely normal cases, both of animals and man, we should conclude that the animal soul at the time of bodily death may return perfectly calmly and naturally into its own roots (as fern-fronds die back in winter), and the whole process may fulfil itself quite simply and graciously and with a minimum of suffering. But this can only be expected to happen in instances where instinctively (as in healthy animals and primitive men) or intentionally (as among a few of mankind) the perfect unity, physical and mental, of the organism has been preserved. In such cases each desire and passion, standing in a close and direct relationship to the spirit or self of the whole organism, is easily and willingly indrawn again at the appointed time; and there is little or no struggle or agony. But in the great masses of mankind—especially in the domains of civilization—where this unity has been lost, it is easily seen that many of the passional elements, loosed from the true service of the informing spirit, carry on a mad and violent career of their own; and to curb these or reduce them to orderly acquiescence and subordination is almost impossible. On the contrary, with the general weakening of the total organism they often break out into greater activity. The ruling passions, "strong in death," push themselves to the fore and tyrannize over the failing or ageing man, and render his actual dissolution stormy and painful; and not only so, but they sometimes generate phantasmal embodiments of themselves which haunt the dying man, or even become visible to outsiders.

Frederick Myers, dealing with this subject,[44] invents the term *psychorrhagy* for this tendency of portions of the *psyche* under certain conditions to break loose from the whole man; and thinks that this process takes place not only at death, but that there are some folk *born* with what he calls a *psychorrhagic diathesis*, who are consequently peculiarly apt for throwing off phantasms of one kind or another. He says:[45]—"That which 'breaks loose' on my hypothesis is not the whole principle of life in the organism; rather it is some psychical element probably of very varying character, and definable mainly by its power of producing a phantasm, perceptible by one or more persons, in some portion or other of space. I hold that this phantasmogenetic effect may be produced either on the mind, and consequently on the brain of another person—in which case he may discern the phantasm somewhere in his vicinity, according to his own mental habit or prepossession—or else directly on a portion of space, 'out in the open,' in which case several persons may simultaneously discern the phantasm in that actual spot."

Myers then proceeds to give a great number of very interesting and extremely well-attested cases of such phantasms, ranging from merely momentary apparitions of persons during their life or at the hour of their death to the persistent haunting of houses over a long period. And I mention this in order to show that there is good authority now for believing it possible not only that phantasms may be generated by the disintegration of the diseased or dying organism, which will haunt the patient himself; but that in cases the psychic elements generating these phantasms may be powerful enough to create a ghostly body which may endure, surviving the earth-body, and manifesting itself to outside observers on occasions for a considerable time.[46]

So much for the fate of the outer personality or animal part. Now with regard to (2), the inner personality or human soul, we may ask, What becomes of that? And the answer particularly interests us, because it is with this section that we—or at least the more thoughtful of mankind generally—identify "ourselves." It is probable that almost any reader of these pages would credit his "I" or "self," not to the one universal Being (to union with whom he may nevertheless distantly aspire), nor to the group of terrestrial desires and interests which we have termed the animal being, but rather to that constellation of nobler character which we have called the human soul. This, he will say, is the self that truly interests, that most deeply represents, me. Tell me, what becomes of that?

I think it is obvious that in the hour of death there are only two directions in which that human soul can turn, in which "we" can turn. We can turn for help either outwards toward the region of the animal self, or inwards toward the central universal self. And I think it equally obvious that the latter direction can alone really supply our need. At first no doubt it may be natural to seek outwards; but now alas! in the hour of dissolution the man discovers that all that region of his nature, in which indeed he has often found comfort before, is becoming involved in the ruin above described. Large portions of his animal faculties are already being torn away—or are sinking into lethargy and sleep. His bodily organs are losing their vitality; some of them have already become useless. His mental faculties—especially the more concrete and external faculties, like the memory of events and names—are becoming disintegrated. True, his general outlook may in cases seem to become wider and more serene as death approaches, and his inner character and personality to become more luminous and gracious; but it is a perilous passage on which he is embarked and in general threatening clouds gather round. The consciousness is painfully invaded by the lesser mentalities which surround it; the ruling passions domineer; silly little habits and tricks, of mind and body, obsess the man; phantoms and delirium overpower, or seek to overpower, him; he is astonished and perturbed to find himself on the fringe of a world in which figures, half-strange, half-familiar, come and go, and force themselves upon him with an odd persistence and a rather terrible kind of intelligence. It requires all his presence of mind to gather himself together, to hold his own, to suppress the rebel rout, and to find amid all the flux something indomitable and sure to which to cling.

There is clearly only one thing to cling to—and this must be insisted on—only that one great redeeming universal Self of which we have spoken: only that superb omnipresent Life which we find in the very central depth of our souls. (And fortunate he who has already so far taken refuge in this, that the wreck and ruin of the visible world and the mortal onset of Death cannot dislodge him!) That alone is fixed and sure; and to that the personal man must turn.

And I think we may say that it is not merely the personal soul's highest duty and best welfare to turn in this direction; but that in a sense and by the law of its nature it must do so. For even in those cases where the man does not recognize this universal Being within, nor consciously believe in and hold on to the same, still is it not true that unconsciously he is very near and very closely related? For all the great qualities which we have already described as characterizing the most intimate human soul, are they not just those which must relate it to the universal Self? I mean such things as Equality—the sense of inner equality with all human and other creatures; Freedom—the sense of freedom from local and material bonds; Indifference—indifference as to fate and destiny; Magnanimity; abounding Charity and Love; dignity; courage; power—all these things, are they not obviously the qualities which dawn upon the personal soul and color it when it is coming into touch with the universal? Are they not the natural 'sign and symbol' of union or partial union with that Self? And more: are there not other things belonging more distinctly to the unconscious and subliminal region (which we shall deal with presently)—I mean such things as deep memory, intuition, clairvoyance, telepathy, prophetic faculty, and so forth—which point to the same conclusion?

The inner personal soul of man is surely already conjoined to the universal, and must cling to it by its very nature. And though the man may not exactly be conscious of this union; though he may hardly really know the depth of his own nature; though, notwithstanding his own splendid qualities of character, some thin film may yet divide him from awareness of the all-redeeming Presence; yet none the less that Presence is there; and is the core and centre of his being.

That being granted, it seems clear that in the disintegration of death the inner personality (whether consciously or unconsciously) will cling to the eternal self within it. And this seems to be the explanation of the part played by Religion in the history of the world, and its close connection with death. The different religions being lame attempts to represent under various guises this one root-fact of the central universal Life, men have at all times clung to the religious creeds and rituals and ceremonials as symbolizing in some rude way the redemption and fulfilment of their own most intimate natures—and this whether consciously understanding the interpretations, or whether (as most often) only doing so in an unconscious or quite subconscious way.

Happy, I say, is the man who has so far consciously taken refuge and identified himself with the great life that the onset of death fails to disturb or dislodge him. For him a wonderful passage is prepared—amazing indeed and bewildering, baffling at times and exhausting, yet by no means dismaying or terrifying. But for the ordinary mortal who has not yet arrived at this—for whom the Presence (beheld perhaps intermittently before) is now clouded and withdrawn from his decisive reach—for such a man it would seem best and most natural simply to gather and compact himself together as firmly as possible, and detaching his mind as well as he can from its earthly entanglements and hindrances, to launch forth boldly, and with such faith and confidence as he can muster, on his strange journey. There is a plant of the Syrian deserts—the Rose of Jericho—about the size of our common daisy plant, and bearing a similar flower, which in dry seasons, when the earth about its roots is turned into mere sand, has the presence of mind to detach itself from its hold altogether and to roll itself into a mere ball—flower, root and all. It is then blown along the plains by the wind and travels away until it reaches some moist and sheltered spot, when it expands again, takes hold on the ground, uplifts its head, and merrily blooms once more. Like the little Rose of Jericho, the human soul has at times to draw in its roots (which we may compare to the animal part) and separate them from their earthly entanglement; even the sun in heaven, which it knows distantly for the source of its life, may be obscured; but compacting itself for the nonce into a sturdy ball, it starts gaily on its far adventure.

May we presume at all to speculate on the soul's actual passage out of this world and its experiences on the way? No doubt there are queer things to be encountered! I think it is obvious that if the soul passes out of this terrestrial world of ours into another state of existence (definite, but quite imperceptible to our present senses) there must be a borderland region in which phenomena occur of an intermediate character—faintly and fitfully perceptible by our present faculties, but lacking in the solidity and regularity of our present world; borderland phenomena in two senses, as being due (*a*) partly to the break-up of our present senses and the present stage of existence, and (*b*) partly to the glimmering perception of forms and figures belonging to a farther stage.

With regard to (*a*), it is of course common for the mind to 'wander,' and for all sorts of phantoms and hallucinations to obsess and cloud it in the last stages of illness; and these vagaries of the mind are no doubt due to or connected with excess or deficiency of circulation in the brain, and morbid physical conditions of one kind or another. But it is possible that a wider and more general view than that may be taken concerning them. I have already referred the reader to the Note at the end of this chapter. All our desires and passions are psychical entities, having a life and consciousness of their own, though affiliated to the total soul within which they work. All our organs and functions are carried on by intelligences, similarly affiliated yet in degree independent. Under normal conditions "we" are unaware of these; entities and intelligences—it is only when they rebel that they come decisively to our notice. In disease, mental and physical, there is rebellion. We become painfully conscious of the independent and often undesired activity of our organs, and of our passions—and so, unfortunately for them, do our friends! In morbid states of mind and body certain functions, certain passions, take on an independent vitality to such a degree that at last they endue a kind of personality and give rise to strings of phantasms which we believe to be real. In dreams, though there is not exactly rebellion, the higher powers of the mental organism being at rest, the lesser functionaries similarly display an extraordinary and impish activity and present us with amazing masquerades of actual life.

What then, we may ask, does probably happen in the moment of death, when the organism has become wasted and enfeebled by disease, and when the nucleus of the man, the inner personality, has compacted itself together into close compass in preparation for its long journey? What happens to all those marginal desires which have chiefly occupied themselves with the affairs of the body or lower mind—those innumerable little spirits and imps which (as we discover in dreams, or by closely watching our waking thoughts) are continually planning and scheming their own little successes and gratifications? What happens to the thousand and one intelligences which carry on the functions and processes of the organism? and whose labors, now that the bodily life is coming to an end, are no more needed? Is there not a danger—or at least a likelihood—of this strange masquerade of dreamland, of these painful obsessions of disease, being repeated with ever-increased intensity? True, that if the organism has been kept so well in hand during life as to cause all outlying passions and desires to weaken and become quiescent simultaneously with the body—or at least to go back quietly into the kennels of a long sleep—like a pack of hounds when the chase is over—then these phantoms, these obsessions, may in that last hour be conspicuous by their absence. But since in the vast majority of cases this is not, and cannot be so, it seems more probable that as a rule the departing soul will make its exit, not only through the perishing bodily part, but through a mass of debris, as it may be called, of the mind (chiefly though perhaps not entirely "the animal mind"), through a cloud of tags and tatters of mentality, thrown off in the final crisis. It seems probable that just as the actual body, bereft at death of its one pervading vitality, breaks out in a mass of corruption or minute multitudinous life, so there is a *tendency*, at any rate, for the lower mind to break out into a strange ghostly rabble—a cloud of phantasms, exhaled and projected from the dying person. Of these phantasms most, no doubt, are only visible to the patient himself (though that does not render them any more agreeable as visitors); others are discernible by clairvoyants present; while others again are distinctly seen even by persons at a distance in space or time—as in the numerous and well-authenticated instances of "wraiths." The picture is not altogether pleasant, but it has a certain general congruity with admitted facts, and with a fairly-accepted body of tradition and theory; and provisionally I suppose we may accept it.

It seems likely, then, that the passage of the inner self, or human soul, out of life and its delivery in another world, *the other side* of death, may very closely correspond to Birth—to the birth of a babe under ordinary conditions *into* this world. Just as the babe, when being born, passes through the lower passages of the body, so the human self at death is expelled inwardly through all the debris and litter of the mind, into another less material and more subtle world than ours. And just as the pangs of childbirth are bad—but they are so mainly beforehand and in preparation, while the actual delivery is swift and a vast relief—so, in cases, the pains and anguish in preparation for death may be great (the squealing of demons torn from their hold on the soul, the cries of intelligences cut off from their coöperative life and source of sustenance in the body, the fears and distress of the animal mind, the yellow fury of the passions, and the death-struggles of the various organs!) yet the final passage itself may be calm and gracious and friendly.

Anyhow, as in other cases of human experience, it would be a mistake to depict this one as by any means uniform in its character. On the contrary, it is probably susceptible of great variety. The Head of a Department (if it becomes necessary for him to leave his post) may find, in one case, that he is turned out, so to speak, with kicks—that he has to run the gauntlet of the execrations of his subordinates; or in another case he may leave amid the expression of every good wish, and along a path made pleasant and easy for him; or again he may go "trailing clouds of glory," and with a retinue of followers behind him, who refuse to remain now that their leader is departing. Some such differences possibly, and we may say probably, present themselves in the passage of death. The experience of childbirth varies to an extraordinary degree. We hear of Indian tribeswomen who only go aside for an hour while their people are on the march, and then rejoin them again at the next halting-place. And who knows but what Death and the preparation for it might be as easy—if only the doctors and the sky-pilots would hurry up and tell us something really useful, instead of spending their time in vivisecting the wretched animals, or in mumbling over ancient creeds?

Now, with regard to the second kind of borderland phenomena, (*b*), the glimmering perception in death of forms and figures or conditions of being belonging to a farther stage of existence: I do not propose at present to dwell upon this matter at any length. But with modern psychical research there has come a good deal of evidence to show that on deathbeds it not at all unfrequently happens that distinct and ardent recognition of departed friends takes place; and though, no doubt, it may seem possible to explain these as cases in which the simple *memory* of a departed friend is very powerfully resuscitated, still this explanation hardly covers a good many cases—such as those for instance in which the dying person was unaware that the friend had died, and yet apparently recognized him as a visitor from the beyond-world.[47] Also of course, modern research has brought forward some amount of testimony in favor of actual communications with the departed through the agency of entranced mediums; so that, though this whole matter is still *sub judice*, we may with fair reason suppose that both in trance-conditions and in the hour of death there are not merely apparitions and phenomena due to disintegrations on *this* side of the border, but also some kind of real communications and manifestations from the other side.

Anyhow, it is clear that each person's experience of death is likely to depend a good deal on the question as to where the centre of gravity of his self-consciousness is placed; and that—as a part of the Art of dying—the object of our endeavor should be to throw (during life) the self-consciousness inward into that part of our being which is durable and immortal in its nature, into that part in which we are united, and feel our union, with other creatures, into that portion where the word itself (self-consciousness) ceases to have a petty and sinister meaning and becomes transformed with a glorious signification. In that case it is indeed likely that the soul may be endowed beforehand with divine vision. It must be our object, by throwing our consciousness always that way, to strengthen the power of the inner soul over the outer personality and all its functions, and at the same time to rivet more and more the hold of that inner soul on the One Self (the source of all vitality and centre of limitless power, if we only understand it so)—so that ultimately the outer and animal personality (though always beautiful in its nature and not to be despised) ceases largely to have an independent and uncoördinated vitality of its own, or to be the scene of uncontrolled activities and conflict, and becomes more the expression and instrument of the inner self: to such a degree indeed that at the dissolution of the body the animal soul, passing into slumber, easily dies down to its deep roots in the human soul, there of course to await its future reawakening, and thus leaving the latter liberated from earth-entanglement and free to start (like the Syrian rose) on its long journey.

In this freeing for the forward journey there must, one would think, be a great sense of joy and satisfaction—even as there must be in the freeing of a May-fly from its water-bred pupa into the glory of air and sunshine. Just as it obviously is (notwithstanding some drawbacks) a joy to the Babe to enter upon its new life, so it may well be that to the dying person—notwithstanding the perils of the change, the fears of the unknown, the parting with friends, the apparent rending of cherished ties—there is a strange joy in shelling off the old husks, and in getting rid of the accumulations and dead rubbish of a lifetime. A thousand and one tiresome old infirmities and bonds of body and mind—now for the first time realized in their true meaning—slip off; and the ship of the soul, "to port and hawser's tie no more returning," departs with a strange thrill and quiver upon its "endless cruise."

The details of this launch and departure we cannot of course ordain. The mode of death is not always within our sphere to determine. Accident may decide, or some hereditary weakness for which the individual can hardly be held responsible. Some diseases are by their nature hard upon the patient; others are kindly in their course. In those that bring great weakness of body there is sometimes an easy passage—the earthly and corporeal part relaxing its hold, while the mind and character become heavenly-clear. In others of an inflammatory nature, or where there is great organic vitality, there may be severe and prolonged struggle. Anyhow, one can imagine the relief when the process is complete. It is not uncommon to experience a strange expansion of the spirit on occasions when the body is seriously weakened by ordinary illness. What must this expansion be when the body finally succumbs—this sense of immensely enlarged life, this impression of sailing forth toward a new and boundless ocean! How strange to stand a moment on the brink of terrestrial mortality, and to be conscious of—to *see*, even with the inner visual power—the shell one has left behind, with all its commonplace and banal surroundings: concrete indeed and material enough, but lying now outside oneself—something almost foreign to one and indifferent, abandoned on the very margin and shore of real life; to stand for a moment; and then to turn and pass inward into that subtle and immense ethereal existence, now to be learnt and explored, which lies within and informs and transfuses all our solid world, and surpasses all its boundaries!

NOTE TO CHAPTER VI

In order not to burden this already rather lengthy chapter with matter which may not be needed, I append here some general considerations for those who have not given much attention to the subject of the various grades of consciousness in the body—considerations tending to show that the various parts and passions of the body and mind have a life and intelligence of their own, and that the whole human organism is a hierarchy (not always perfectly harmonious) of psychic entities.

We generally allow of course that our central or dominant selves are alive and conscious (though no doubt we use those epithets with a rather sad vagueness). But having allowed that, the extraordinary phenomena of variable and alternating personality compel us to admit that there may be many such centres within one person, each of which though now buried may in its turn become dominant and take conscious lead, and which must therefore be credited with life and intelligence (even if an alien life and intelligence to "our own"). Even the most ordinary brain-centres are in the habit of carrying on whole departments of the bodily organization with an independent intelligence of their own, and are sometimes liable under the influence of some excitement (like drink, or religion, or some enthusiasm) to take possession of the whole man and transform him into another creature—exhibiting in doing so a strange degree of invasive vitality and alertness. It is quite certain that the myriad microscopic cells of the body are alive, each with its own little particular life; and the more one studies these cells the more difficult it is not to credit them each, in their degree, with a particular consciousness or intelligence. And each body-organ again, composed of a congeries or colony of body-cells, has a life of its own on and beyond that of its component cells, and exhibits curious signs too of intelligence and emotion, which often (especially in sickness) affect the moods and thoughts of the entire man.

The whole of the subconscious world, in fact—that world which only occasionally breaks through into the upper consciousness—must be allowed to be alive, and in its various degrees methodical and calculating. This is well seen in the phenomena of dreams and of hypnotism, in both of which the most acute and diabolical ingenuity is often shown—as of weird imps working in dark chambers of the brain quite unbeknown to their supposed lord and master; or in the extraordinary phenomena of trance and "automatic" speaking and writing; or in telepathy and clairvoyance; or again in the craftiness of utter lunatics; or in the strange evasions and mental dodgery which (as just hinted) are induced by diseases of certain organs; or in the phenomena of mental healing, where an appeal to the subconscious intelligence in any and every corner of the body is often followed by extraordinary response; or in the subtle instinctive knowledge and perception of babes, and of animals, long before *self*-consciousness has developed; or again, in the sly cunning of ancient dotards; or in the complex bodily reflexes carried on perfectly unknown to ourselves during life; or in the continued functioning of some of the organs after death. In all these cases, and in scores of others not mentioned, it is clear that the majority of the processes of the human system are carried on by minor intelligences. They are indeed carried on by *crowds* of minor intelligences—to which we accord the epithet "automatic," and which no doubt we regard as mechanical, as long, that is, as they work smoothly and without friction and opposition. But when they do not do so, when pain, disease and lunacy cut in—when a violent burn sets the epithelial cells screaming, and the scream comes into our consciousness as the vibration of pain; when a diseased liver twists the events of life and the faces of our friends into malignant shape and mien; when lust and hypochondria people the mind with phantoms; and drink makes all the functions mad—then we say we are "possessed with devils," then we recognize, if only on the dark side, the pervading intelligence or intelligences of the body.

It is like the Head of a Department, as I have said, whose subordinate officials are working under him agreeably and harmoniously. As long as that is the case, he may have in his mind a general outline of the working of the Department. He probably is ignorant of most of the details; he certainly does not know personally many of his subordinates, but he superintends the working of the whole. Presently, however, occurs something of a strike or *émeute*; whereupon he discovers that vast numbers of his men are intelligently discussing questions or problems of whose existence he was almost ignorant; personalities appear before him whom, before, he knew at most only by name; and they argue their case with an acumen and vitality which surprises him. For the first time, in this revolt of his department, he comes to realize the amount of intelligent activity which is at work within it, beneath the surface. So it is with us in the case of disease. In health we have no trouble, unity prevails. As long as "we" are on top, and the intelligences which carry on the body are working on friendly terms with us, their minds do not intrude into our realm, and we are practically unaware of them. But when through our mismanagement or other cause dissension breaks out, then indeed we realize what kind of forces they are with which we have to deal, and of what a wonderful hierarchy of intelligences the body is composed.[48]

CHAPTER VII

IS THERE AN AFTER-DEATH STATE?

IN the last chapter Death was compared to Birth, and it was said that probably the passage of the human soul into another world, *on the other side of death*, exactly corresponded to Birth—to the birth of a babe into this world. And certainly, seeing these apparent movements *into* the visible and *away* from it again, it is very natural to assume that there *is* such another and hidden world, and to speculate upon its nature.

But it may fairly be asked, is there after all any reason for supposing that there is a definite state of existence of any kind on that side? Is it not quite likely that there is only vacancy and nothingness, or at best a mere formless pulp (of ether and electrons, or whatever it may be) out of which souls are born and into which they return again at death? It is this question which I propose to discuss in the present chapter.

Historically speaking, we know of course that early and primitive folk, letting their imaginations loose, peopled that 'other side' and rather promiscuously, with all sorts of fairy beings and phantom processions. Giant grizzly bears, divine jackals, elves, dwarfs, satans, holy ghosts, lunar pitris, flaming sun-gods, and so forth, ruled and raged behind the curtain—in front of which the shivering mortal stood. But as time went on, the growing exactitude of thought and science made it more and more impossible to idly accept these imaginings; and it may be said that about the middle of last century these cosmogonies—for the more thoughtful among the populations of the Western world—finally perished, and gave place for the most part to a simple negative attitude. It was allowed that intelligences and personalities (human and animal) moved on *this* side of the veil, and were plainly distinguishable as operating in the actual world; but they, it was held, were more or less isolated and probably accidental products of a mechanical universe. That mechanical arrangement of atoms, and so forth, which we could now largely map out and measure, and which doubtless in the future we should be able completely to define—that was the universe, and somehow or other included everything. One of its properties was that it would run down like a clock, and would eventuate in time in a cold sun and a dead earth—and there was an end of it! Any intelligent existence behind or on the other side of this veil of mechanism was too problematical to be worth discussing; in all probability on that side was mere nothingness and vacancy.

Such, very roughly stated, was the attitude of the fairly intelligent and educated man about fifty years ago, but since that time the outgrowths of science and human inquiry have been so astounding as to leave that position far behind. The obvious signs of intelligence in the minutest cells, almost invisible to the naked eye, the very mysterious arcana of growth in such cells (partly described in a former chapter), the myriad action of similarly intelligent microbes, the strange psychology of plants, and the equally strange psychic sensitiveness (apparently) of *metals*, the sudden transformations and variations both of plants and animals, the existence of the X and N rays of light, and of countless other vibrations of which our ordinary senses render no account, the phenomena of radium and radiant matter, the marvels of wireless telegraphy, the mysterious facts connected with hypnotism and the subliminal consciousness, and the certainty now that telepathic communication can take place between human beings thousands of miles apart—all these things have convinced us that the subtlest forces and energies, totally unmeasurable by our instruments, and saturated or at least suffused with intelligence, are at work all around us. They have convinced us that gloomy phrases about cold suns and dead earths are mere sentiment and nonsense. Cold worlds there may certainly be, but nothing is more certain than that worlds on worlds, and spheres on spheres, stretch behind and beyond the actually seen—spheres so microscopic as to totally elude us, or so vast and cosmic as to elude, spheres of vibration which elude, spheres of other senses than ours, spheres aerial, ethereal, magnetic, mental, subliminal. The iris-veil of our ordinary existence may truly be rent, but the visible world, the world we know, is no longer now a film on the surface of an empty bubble, but a curtain concealing a vast and teeming life, reaching down endless, in layer on layer, into the very heart of the universe. And whereas, in the former time of which I have been speaking, we might have agreed that life could not well continue after the death of the body, to-day we should, as a first guess, be inclined to think that life is *more* full and rich on the other side of death than on this side. "I do not doubt," says Whitman, "that from under the feet and beside the hands and face I am cognizant of, are now looking faces I am not cognizant of, calm and actual faces—I do not doubt interiors have their interiors, and exteriors have their exteriors, and that the eyesight has another eyesight, and the hearing another hearing, and the voice another voice."

We come, then, to this problem of Death and Birth in a similarly modified spirit, and with a predisposition to believe that they do really indicate passages from one definite world or plane or region of existence to another. And here is the place to point out, and to guard ourselves against, a common error in the use of the word Death. Death is not a *state*. There may be an after-death state; but death itself is the *passage* into that state, or—better—the passage out of the present state. So Birth is not a state. There may be a pre-birth state; but birth itself is the passage into the present state. Either we pass through death into another life and condition of being; or else we are extinguished. In the former case there is clearly no *state* of death; and in the latter case there is no such state—because there is no self to *be* dead or to know itself dead. As Lucretius says,[49] endeavoring to disabuse man of the fear of the grave:—

> "So to be mortal fills his mind with dread,
>
> Forgetting that in real death can be
>
> No self, to mourn that other self as dead,
>
> Or stand and weep at death's indignity."

Birth and Death, then, we may look upon as two contrary movements, to some degree complementary and balancing each other; and it is possible that thus, from consideration of the one, we may be able to infer things about the other. One such thing that we may be able to infer is that Love presides over, or is intimately associated with, both movements.

The connection of Love with Birth is of course obvious. In some profound yet hidden way, almost throughout creation, the birth or generation of one creature is connected with the precedent love and sex-fusion of two others. And the connection of Love with Death, though not so prominent, can similarly almost everywhere be traced. The whole of poetry in literature teems with this subject; and so does the poetry of Nature! If we are to believe the Garden of Eden story, Love and Death came into the world together; and it certainly is curious that in the age-long evolution of animal forms the same thing seems to have happened. The Protozoa at first, propagating by simple division, were endued with a kind of immortality. But then came a period when a pair found they could enter into a joint life of renewed fecundity by fusing with each other. They literally died in each other, and rose again in a numerous progeny; so that love and death were simultaneous and synonymous. Sometimes parturition and death were simultaneous. The mother-cell perished in the very act of giving birth to her brood. Then again came the aggregation of cells into living groups—the formation of 'colonial' organisms; and it was then that distinctive sex-differentiation and sex-organs appeared, and with the capacity of sex also the capacity of death through the disruption of the colony. Everywhere love is associated with death. The expenditure of seed in the male animal is an incipient death; the formation of the seed vessel, and the glory and color of the flowering plant, are already the signs of its decay. "Both Weismann and Goette," say Geddes and Thomson,[50] "note how many insects (locusts, butterflies, ephemerids, and so forth) die a few hours after the production of ova. The exhaustion is fatal, and the males are also involved. In fact, as we should expect from the katabolic temperament, it is the males which are especially liable to exhaustion.... Every one is familiar with the close association of love and death in the common May-flies. Emergence into winged liberty, the love-dance, and the process of fertilization, the deposition of eggs, and the death of both parents, are often the crowded events of a few hours. In higher animals, the fatality of the reproductive sacrifice has been greatly lessened, yet death may tragically persist, even in human life, as the direct Nemesis of love."

George Macdonald, in one of his books (*Phantastes*, vol. i. p.), feigns a race of beings, for whom death is not so much the 'nemesis' of love, as its natural and inevitable outcome. Seized by a great love, too great for mortal expression, "looking *too* deep into each other's eyes," they (with great presence of mind, it must be said!) breathe their souls out in death, and so take their departure to another world. Heine touches the same note in his poem, the "Asra":—

"Ich bin aus Jemen,

Und mein stamm sind jene Asra,

Welche sterben wenn sie lieben."

And scores of scarcely noticed paragraphs in our daily papers, brief tales of single or double suicide, present us with a dim outline of how—even in the mean conditions and surroundings of our modern days—every now and then there comes to one or other a longing, a passion, and a revelation of a desire so intense, that, breaking the bounds of a useless life, it demands swift utterance in death.

Some deep and profound suggestion there is in all this—some hint of a life whose very form and nature is love, and which finds its deliverance and nativity only through the abandonment of the body—even as our ordinary life, conceived in love, finds its delivery into this world through what we call birth. At the very least it suggests that Death may have a great deal more to do with Love, and may be more deeply allied to it than is generally supposed. And it may suggest that the two things, being in some sense the most important occupations of the human race, should be frankly recognized as such, and should both be accordingly prepared for.

Another thing, about which we may be able to infer something from the analogy between Birth and Death, is the fate of the soul at death. If we can trace in any way the relation of the soul to the body at the time of the first appearance of the latter, that may shed light on the relation which will hold at its disappearance. We cannot certainly define very strictly what we mean by the word 'soul'; but we are all very well aware that associated with our bodies, and in some sense pervading them with its intelligence, is a conscious (as well as subconscious) being which we call the self or soul; and we are all puzzled at times to understand what is the relation between this and the body. Now we have seen (ch. ii.) the genesis of the body from a single fertilized cell or germ almost microscopic in size, and its growth by continual and myriadfold division into, say, a human form; and we have seen that every cell in the perfect and final form—every cell, of eye, or liver, or of any part or organ—is there by linear descent or division from that first cell, though variously adapted and differentiated during the process. We are therefore almost compelled to conclude that that intelligent self (conscious or subconscious) which we are so distinctly aware of as associated with our mature bodies was there also, associated with the first germ.[51] It may not truly have been outwardly manifest or unfolded into evidence at that primitive stage. It could not well be. But it was there, even in its totality, and unless it had been there, we could not now be what we are. The conscious and subconscious self has been within us all along, unfolding and manifesting itself with the unfoldment and development of the body; and indeed to all appearances guiding that development. And more, we may fairly say—having regard to the mode of development of the tissue—that it dwells even in its entirety within every normal and healthy cell of our present bodies, and is the formative essence thereof.

Let me give an illustration. Sometimes in the morning you may see a bush glittering all over with dewdrops; every leaf has such a tiny jewel hanging from it. If now you look you will see in each dewdrop a miniature picture of the far landscape. Or, to take a closer illustration, some shrubs have, embedded in the very tissue of their leaves, tiny transparent and lens-like glands which yield to close scrutiny similar miniatures of the world beyond. Exactly, then, like these plants, we may think of the whole human body as trembling in light—each cell containing (if we could but see it!) a luminous image of the presiding genius or self of the body.

The question is often asked: *Where* is the self? does it reside in the head, or in the heart, or perhaps in the liver? is it an aural halo pervading and surrounding the body, or is it a single microscopic cell far hidden in the interior, or is it an invisible atom? Here apparently is the answer. It animates *every* cell. It pervades the whole body, and seeks expression in every part of it. Some cells, as we have said before, are differentiated so as to express especially *this* faculty, others to express especially *that*; but the human soul or self stands behind them all. Look at a baby's face, and its growing sparkling expression—an individual being coming newly into the world, obviously seeking, feeling, tentatively finding its way forward—every morning a thinnest veil falling from its features! Playing through the whole body, is an intelligence, seeking expression. Helen Keller, the girl both deaf and blind, describes most graphically her agonizing experiences at the age of six or seven, when her growing powers of body and mind demanded the expression which her physical disabilities so cruelly denied. "The desire to express myself grew,"[52] she says; "the few signs I used became less and less adequate, and my failures to make myself understood were invariably followed by outbursts of passion. I felt as if invisible hands were holding me, and I made frantic efforts to free myself." And then most touching, the description of her relief, "the thrill of surprise, the joy of discovery," when she at last, about the age of ten, was able to utter her first intelligible words. In some degree like Helen Keller's is perhaps the experience of every babe that is born into the world.

It seems to me, therefore, that each person is practically compelled to think of his 'self' as moving behind or as associated with or animating every cell in the healthy body; and as having been so associated with the first germ of the same, even though that was a thing well-nigh invisible to the naked eye. You were there, you are there now, at the root of your bodily life. You may not, certainly, except at moments, be distinctly conscious of this your complete relation to the body; but, as we have already said, the term self must be held to include the large subconscious tracts which occasionally flash up into consciousness, and which, when they do so flash, almost always confirm this relation; nor must we lose from sight the still more deeply buried physiological or animal soul, whose operations we seem to be able to trace from earliest days, guiding all the complex of organic growth and development, and apparently conscious in its own way with a very wonderful sort of intelligence.[53]

All this compels us, I think, not only to picture to ourselves the mental self or soul as associated with the body, and taking part in its development from the first inception of the latter; but also to picture that self as in its entirety considerably *greater* and more extensive than the ordinary conscious self, and even as greater than any bodily expression or manifestation which it succeeds in gaining. We are compelled, I think, to regard the real self as at all times only *partially* manifested.

I think this latter point is obvious; for when, and at what period in life, is manifestation complete? Certainly not in babyhood, when the faculties are only unfolding; certainly not in old age, when they are decaying and falling away. Is it, then, in maturity and middle life? But during all that period the output of expression and character in a man is constantly changing; and which of all these changes of raiment is completely representative? Do we not rather feel that to express our real selves *every* phase from childhood through maturity even into extreme old age ought to be taken into account? Nay, more than that; for have we not—perhaps most of us—a profound feeling and conviction that there are elements deep down in our natures, which never have been expressed, and never can or will be expressed in our present and actual lives? Do we not all feel that our best is only a fraction of what we want to say? And what must we think of the strange facts of multiple personality? Do they not suggest that our real self has facets so opposite, so divergent, that for a long time they may appear quite disconnected with each other; until ultimately (as has happened in actual cases) they have been visibly reconciled and harmonized in a new and more perfect character?

With regard to this view that the real person is so much greater than his visible manifestation, Frederick Myers and Oliver Lodge have used the simile of a ship. And it is a fine one. A ship gliding through the sea has a manifestation of its own, a very partial one, in the waterworld below—a ponderous hull moving in the upper layers of that world—a form encrusted with barnacles and sea-weed. But what denizen of the deep could have any inkling or idea of the real life of that ship in the aerial plane—the glory of sails and spars trimmed to the breeze and glancing in the sun, the blue arch of heaven flecked with clouds, the leaping waves and the boundless horizon around the ship as she speeds onward, the ingenious provision for her voyage, the compass, the helmsman and the captain directing her course? Surely (except in moments of divination and inspiration) we have little idea of what we really are! But there *are* such moments—moments of profound grief, of passionate love, of great and splendid angers and enthusiasms which dart light back into the farthest recesses of our natures and astonish us with the vision they disclose. And (perhaps more often) there are moments which disclose the wonder-self in others. If we do not recognize (which is naturally not easy!) our own divinity, it is certain that we cannot really *love* without discovering a divine being in the loved one—a being remote, resplendent, inaccessible, who calls for and indeed demands our devotion, but of whom the mortal form is most obviously a mere symbol and disguise. There are times when this strange illumination falls on people at large, and we see them as gods walking: when we look even on the tired overworked mother in the slum, and her face is shining like heaven; or on the ploughboy in the field with his team, and see the mould and the material of ancient heroes. Yet of what is really nearest to them all the time these folk say nothing, and we are astonished to find them haggling over halfpence or seriously troubled about wire-worms. It is as if a play, or some kind of deliberate mystification, were being carried on—with disguises a little too thin. We see, as plain as day—and nothing can contravene our conclusion—that it is only a fraction of the real person that is concerned.

Your self, then, I say—covering by that word not only all that you and your friends usually include in it, but probably a good deal more—existed, with all its potentialities and capacities even in association with the first primitive germ of your present body.[54] That germ was microscopic in size, and its inner workings and transformations were ultra-microscopic in character. We do not know whence they originated; and whether we think of the soul which was associated with them as ultra-microscopic in *its* nature or as fourth-dimensional does not much matter. We only perceive that it, the soul, must have been there, in an unseen world of some kind, pushing forward toward its manifestation in the visible.[55] I do not think we can well escape this conclusion.

But if we conclude that the soul existed before Birth, or, more properly, at or before conception, in some such invisible world, then that it should so exist after Death is equally possible, nay, probable. For after conception, by continual multiplication and differentiation of cells, the soul framed for itself organs of expression and manifestation, and thus gradually came into our world of sight and sense and ordinary intelligence; and so, by some reverse process, we may suppose that in decay and death the soul gradually loses these organs and their coördination, and retires into the invisible. Whatever the nature of this invisible may be—whether, as I say, a world of things too minute for human perception, or too vast for the same, or whether a world which eludes us by the simple artifice of everywhere and in everything running parallel to the things of the world—only in another dimension imperceptible to us—in any case it seems reasonable to suppose that the soul is still *there*, fulfilling its nature and its destiny, of which its earth-life has only been one episode.[56]

And if the apparent loss of consciousness (the loss of the ordinary consciousness at any rate) which often takes place during the death-change, seems to point to extinction and not to continuance, I think that that need not disturb us. For in sleep, in our nightly sleep, the same suspension of the ordinary consciousness takes place, as we very well know; yet all the time the subconsciousness is functioning away—sorting out sounds, bidding us wake for some, allowing us to sleep through others, discriminating disturbances, carrying on the physiologies of the body, posting sentinels in the reflexes—and guarding us from harm—till untired in the morning it knits together again the ravelled thread of the ordinary consciousness and renews our waking activities. And if this happens in our ordinary and nightly sleep, it seems at any rate possible that something similar may happen in death. Indeed there is much evidence to show that while at the hour of death the supraliminal consciousness often passes into a state of quiescence or abeyance, the subliminal, or at any rate some portion of the subliminal, becomes unusually active. Audition grows strangely keen—so much so that it is sometimes difficult to tell whether the things heard have been apprehended by extension of the ordinary faculty or whether by a species of clairaudience. Vision similarly passes into clairvoyance, the patient becomes extraordinarily sensitive to telepathic influences, and knows what is going on at a distance;[57] and not only so, but he radiates influences *to* a distance. All the phenomena of wraiths and dying messages, now so well substantiated—of apparitions and impressions projected with force at the moment of death into the minds of distant friends—prove clearly the increased activity and vitality (one may say) of the subliminal self at that time; and this points, as I say, not to extinction and disorganization, but perhaps to the transfer of consciousness more decisively into hidden regions of our being. One hears sometimes of a dying person who, prevented from departure by the tears and entreaties of surrounding friends, cries out "Oh! *let* me die!" and one remembers the case, above mentioned, of the apparently dead mother who, so to speak, called herself back to life by the thought of her orphaned children. Such cases as these do not look like loss of continuity; rather they look as if a keen intelligence were still there, well aware of its earth-life, but drawn onward by an inevitable force, and passing into a new phase, of swifter subtler activity in perhaps a more ethereal body.

That the human soul does pass through great transformations—moultings and sloughings and metamorphoses—and so forward from one stage to another, we know from the facts of life. Physiologically the body takes on a new phase at birth, and another at weaning and teething, and another at puberty, and another in age at the 'change of life,' and so on; and transformations of the soul or inner life (some of them very remarkable) are associated with these outer phases. The last great bodily change is obviously accompanied—as we have just indicated—by the development or extension of hidden psychic powers. What exactly that final transformation may be, we can only at present speculate; but we can see that, like the others, when it arrives it has already become very necessary and inevitable. At every such former stage—whether it be birth, or teething, or puberty, or what not—there has been constriction or strangulation. The growing inner life has found its conditions too limited for it, and has burst forth into new form and utterance. In this final change the bodily conditions altogether seem to have grown too limited. With an irresistible impulse and an agonizing joy of liberation the soul sweeps out, or is fearfully swept, into its new sphere. Sometimes doubtless the passage is one of pain and terror; far more often, and in the great majority of cases, it is peaceful and calm, with a deep sense of relief; occasionally it is radiant with ecstasy, as if the new life already cast its splendor in advance.[58]

Yes, we cannot withhold the belief that there is an after-death state—a state which in a sense is present with us, and has been present, all our lives; but which—for reasons that at present we can only vaguely apprehend—has been folded from our consciousness.

CHAPTER VIII

THE UNDERLYING SELF

ALLOWING, then, the great probability of the existence of an after-death state, and of a survival of some kind, the question further arises: Is that survival in any sense personal or individual? or does it belong to some, so to speak, formless region, either below or above personality? It is conceivable of course that there may be survival of the outer and beggarly elements of the mind, below personality; or it is conceivable that the deepest and most central core of the man may survive, far beyond and above personality; but in either case the *individual* existence may not continue. The eternity of the All-soul or Self of the universe is, I take it, a basic fact; it is from a certain point of view obvious; we have already discussed it, and, as far as this book is concerned, it is treated so much as an axiom that to argue further without it would be useless. That being granted, it follows that if the soul of each human being roots down ultimately into that All-self, the core of each soul *must* partake of the eternal nature. But as far as it does so it *may* be beyond all reach or remembrance or recognition of personality.

Such a conclusion—whatever force of conviction may accompany it—is certainly not altogether satisfactory. I remember that once—in the course of conversation with a lady on this very subject—she remarked that though she thought there would be a future life she did not believe in the continuance of individuality. "What do you believe in, then?" said I. "Oh," she replied, "I think we shall be a sort of Happy Mass!" And I have always since remembered that expression.

But though the idea of a happy mass has its charms, it does not, as I say, quite satisfy either our feelings or our intelligence. There is a desire for something more, and there is a perception that Differentiation and Individuation represent a great law—a law so great as probably to extend even to the ultimate modes of Being. And though a vague generality of this kind cannot stand in the place of strict reasoning or observation, it may make us feel that personal survival is at any rate possible, and that a certain amount of speculation on the subject is legitimate.

At the same time we have to bear in mind that the subject altogether is a very complex one, and that we have to move only slowly, if we want to move forward at all, and to avoid having to retrace our steps. We must not too serenely assume, for instance, that we at all know what we are! We have already (ch. v.) analyzed to some degree the constitution of the human being, and found it complicated enough in its successive planes of development. We have now to remember that—at least on the two middle planes, those of the human soul and the animal soul—there is another subdivision to be made, namely between that part which is conscious and that which is only subconscious; so that further complications inevitably arise. We may not only have to consider, as in the chapter referred to, which of these planes may possibly carry survival with it, but again whether such survival may be in the conscious region, or only in the subliminal or subconscious. This chapter will be largely occupied with a consideration of the subliminal or underlying portion of the self, and it will be seen that that is probably of immense extent and variety of content compared with the surface or conscious portion; but it will also be seen that there is no strict line of demarcation between the two, and that a continual interchange betwixt them is taking place, so that for the present at any rate it is safest to give the word 'self' its widest scope and make it include both portions and every mental faculty, rather than limit its application.

In attacking the subject, then, of the Survival of the Self, I suppose our first question ought to be: What is the test of survival, what do we mean by it? And to this, I imagine, the answer is, Continuity of Consciousness. This would seem to be the only satisfying definition. Consciousness is necessary in some form or other, as the base and evidence of our existence; and continuity in some degree is also necessary, in order to link our experiences together, as it were into one chain. Continuity, however, need not be absolute. The chain of consciousness may apparently be broken by sleep, or it may be broken by a dose of chloroform, or by a blow on the head; but it may be re-knit and resumed. It may pass from the supraliminal state to the subliminal, and again emerge on the surface. It may even be discontinuous; but as long as Memory bridges the intervals we get the *sense* of continuity of life or personality.[59] Supposing a body of memories—of life say in some village of ancient Egypt—suddenly opened up in one's mind, as vivid and consistent and enduring as one's ordinary memory of childhood days, it would be natural to conclude that one really had pre-existed in that village; it would be difficult not to make that inference. And similarly if at some future time, and in far other than our present surroundings, the memory of this one's earth-life should emerge again, vivid and personal as now, the being thus having that memory would, we suppose, conclude that he had once lived this life here on earth.

Thus Memory would be the arbiter of survival and of the continuity (on the whole) of consciousness. Frederick Myers, indeed, goes so far as to define consciousness as that which is "potentially memorable"[60]—thus suggesting that memory is a necessary accompaniment of any psychic state to which we can venture to give the name of consciousness.

It may indeed seem precarious to rest our test of survival on so notoriously fallible, and even at times fallacious, a thing as Memory; but one does not see that there is anything better, or that there is any alternative! The memory may not be continuously enduring and operative; but if at any future time one should be persuaded of having survived from this present life, it must, one would say, be by memory in some form or other, *of* this present life. And it must be remarked that though memory is fitful and fallible, these epithets apply mainly to the supraliminal memory, to that superficial memory which we make use of by conscious effort, and which often fails us in the moment of need. Deep below this we dimly perceive, and daily are becoming more persuaded of, the existence of vast and permanent but latent stores, which from time to time emerge into manifestation; and more and more our psychologists are inclining to think that the supraliminal self gains its memories by tapping these stores, and that its lapses and oblivions are more due to failure in the tapping process than to any failure of the memory stores themselves. Indeed not a few psychologists are now asking whether it is not likely that *every* psychic experience carries memory with it, and so is preserved in the great storehouse.

I have already, in the last chapter, spoken of the so-called subliminal self as, among other things, a wonderful storehouse of memory; and I propose now to occupy a few pages with the more detailed consideration of the nature of that self; because, as we are discussing the question of survival, our discussion, as I have just said, ought obviously to include the under as well as the upper strata of consciousness. We cannot very well confine our meaning and our inquiry to the little brain-self only, and leave out of consideration the great self of the emotions and impulses—of genius, love, enthusiasm, and so forth.[61] No, we must include both—the more intimate, though more hidden, self, as well as the self of the façade and the front window.

This hidden self is indeed an astounding thing, whose extent and complexity grows upon us as investigation proceeds. For when the term 'subliminal' was first used it had apparently a fairly simple connotation—as of some *one* obscure and unexplored chamber of the mind; but now instead of a single chamber it would seem rather some vast house or palace at whose door we stand, with many chambers and corridors—some dark and underground, some spacious and well lighted and furnished, some lofty with extensive outlook and open to the sky; and the modern psychologists are puzzling themselves to find suitable names for all these new domains—which indeed they cannot satisfactorily do, seeing they know so little of their geography!

I can only attempt here—very roughly I am afraid, and unsystematically—to point out *some* of the properties and qualities of the underlying or hidden or subconscious self—whichever term we may like to use. In the first place, its memory appears to be little short of perfect, and at any rate to our ordinary intelligence and estimate, nothing short of marvellous. When a servant girl, who can neither read nor write, reproduces, in her wandering speech during a nervous fever, whole sentences of Latin, Greek, and Hebrew, which she could not possibly understand, and which had only fallen quite casually on her ears years before from the lips of an old scholar (who used to recite passages to himself as he walked up and down a room adjoining the kitchen in which the girl at that time worked[62]); we perceive that the under or latent memory *may* catch and retain for a lengthy period, and with strange accuracy, the most fleeting and apparently superficial impressions. When Dr. Milne Bramwell instructs a hypnotized subject to make a cross on a bit of paper exactly 20, minutes after the giving of the order; and the patient, having of course emerged from the hypnotic sleep, and gone about her daily work, and having no conscious remembrance of the command, does nevertheless at the expiration of the stated number of days and minutes take a piece of paper and make the said cross upon it,[63] we can only marvel both at the persistence and accuracy of memory which the subliminal being displays, and at the strict command which this being may exercise in its silent way over the actions of the supraliminal self. When we are repeatedly told that in the moment of drowning, people remember every action and event of their past life, though we may doubt the exact force of the word 'every,' we cannot but be convinced that an enormous and astounding resurgence of memory does take place,[64] and we cannot but suspect that the memorization is somehow on a different plane of consciousness from the usual one, being simultaneous and in mass instead of linear and successive. Or when, again, a 'calculating boy' or prodigy of quite tender years on being asked to find the cube-root of 31,, instantly says , or being given the number 17, immediately remarks that it consists of the factors × 53,[65] we are reduced to the alternative suppositions, either that the boy's subconscious self works out these sums with a perfectly amazing rapidity, or that it has access to stores of memory and knowledge quite beyond the experience of the life-time concerned. In all these cases, and hundreds and thousands of others which have been observed, the memory of the subliminal self—whether manifested through hypnotism, or in sleep or dreams, or in other ways—seems to exceed in range and richness, as well as in rapidity, the memory of the supraliminal self; and indeed Myers goes so far as to say that the deeper down one penetrates below the supraliminal, the more perfect is the remembrance: that, in cases where one can reach various planes of memory in the same subject, "it is the memory furthest from waking life whose span is the widest, whose grasp of the organism's upstored impressions is the most profound."[66] This is, I think, a very important conclusion, and one to which we may recur later.

But the hidden being within us does not show this extraordinary command of mental processes merely in technical matters. Its powers extend far deeper, into such regions as those of Genius and Prophecy. The wonderful flashes of intuition, the complex combinations of ideas, which at times leap fully formed and with a kind of authority into the field of man's waking consciousness, obviously proceed from a deep intelligence of some kind, lying below, and are the product of an immensely extended and rapid survey of things, brought to a sudden focus. They yield us the finest flowers of Art; and some at any rate of the most remarkable instances of Prediction. For though there may be—and probably is—a purely clairvoyant prophetic gift, freed as it were from the obscuration of Time, yet it cannot be doubted that much or most of prophecy is simply very swift and conclusive inference derived from very extensive observation.

These flashes and inspirations are clearly not the product of the conscious brain; they are felt by the latter to come from beyond it. They are, in the language of Myers, "uprushes from the subliminal self." And even beyond them there are things which come from the same source—there are splendid enthusiasms, and overwhelming impulses of self-sacrifice, as well as mad and dæmonic passions.

Yet again, it is not merely command of *mental* processes that the subconscious being displays, but of the bodily powers and processes too. Intelligent itself to the marvellous degrees already indicated, it is evident also that its intelligence penetrates and ordains the whole body. Every one has heard of the *stigmata* of the Crucifixion appearing on the hands and feet of some religious devotee, as in the celebrated case of Louise Lateau. Dr. Briggs of Lima once told a hypnotized patient that "a red cross would appear on her chest every Friday during a period of four months"—and obediently the mark appeared.[67] A whisper in such cases is often sufficient; and the latent power swiftly but effectually modifies all the complex activities and functions of the organism to produce the desired result. What an extraordinary combination of elaborate intelligence and detailed organizing power must here be at work! And the same in the quite common yet very remarkable cases of mental healing, with which we are all now familiar!

Sometimes again—quite apart from any oral suggestion or apparent outside influence—we find the subjective being taking most decisive command of a person's faculties and actions. This happens, for instance, in somnambulism, when the sleepwalker perhaps passes along the narrow and perilous ridge of a roof or wall with perfect balance and sureness of foot—adjusting a hundred muscles in the most delicate way, and yet with total unconsciousness as far as the supraliminal self is concerned. Or it happens sometimes—even more remarkably—to people in full possession of their waking faculties, at some moment when extreme danger threatens to overwhelm them. John Muir in his *The Mountains of California*,[68] describes how when scaling the very precipitous face of a cliff he found himself completely baffled, at a great height from the ground, and unable to proceed either up or down. He was seized with panic and a trembling in every limb, and was on the point of falling, when suddenly a perfect calm and assurance took possession of him, and somehow—he never quite knew how—with an astonishing agility and sure-footedness he completed the ascent, and was saved. "I seemed suddenly to become possessed of a new sense. The other Self—bygone experiences, Instinct or Guardian Angel, call it what you will—came forward and assumed control. My trembling muscles became firm again, every rift and flaw in the rock was seen as through a microscope, and my limbs moved with a positiveness and precision with which I seemed to have nothing at all to do. Had I been borne aloft upon wings, my deliverance could not have been more complete."

Mæterlinck, in his chapter on "The Psychology of Accident" (in *Life and Flowers*), describes how in the nerve-commotion of danger, Instinct, "a rugged, brutal, naked, muscular figure," rushes to the rescue. "With a glance that is surer and swifter than the onrush of the peril, it takes in the situation, then and there unravels all its details, issues and possibilities, and in a trice affords a magnificent, an unforgettable spectacle of strength, courage, precision, and will, in which unconquered life flies at the throat of death." And similar instances—of instinctive presence of mind, and an almost miraculous development of faculty in extreme danger—are within the knowledge of most people. The subliminal being steps in quite decisively, and the ordinary conscious mind *feels* that another power is taking over the reins.

But there is another faculty of the subjacent self which must not be passed over, and which is very important—I mean the image-forming power. This is one of the prime faculties of all intelligent beings, lying at the very root of creation; and it is a faculty possessed to an extreme and impressive degree by the self "behind the scenes." I have discussed this subject generally at some length in my book *The Art of Creation*, and need not repeat the matter here, except to allude to a few points. The image-forming faculty is a natural attribute of the conscious mind, in all perhaps but the lowest grades of evolution; at any rate it is difficult to think of a mind at all like ours *without* this faculty. This faculty is most active when the mind is withdrawn into itself, in quietude. In his study or when burning the midnight oil the writer's brain teems, or is supposed to teem, with images! But in sleep the image-forming activity is even greater. It then shows itself in the subconscious mind, in the world of dreams, whose bodiless creations are more vivid and energetic than those of our waking hours, and have a strange sense of *reality* about them. But again, in the deeper sleep of trance still more vivid images are produced. A young student hypnotized imagines himself to be Napoleon, then to be Garibaldi, then to be an old woman of ninety, then to be a mere child. He acts the parts of these characters, imitates their handwriting, their voices, issues proclamations to his soldiers in the name of the first two, assumes the shaky penmanship of childhood and of old age; and all in the course of half-an-hour or so.[69] The images thus formed in the deep trance of the young man are so vivid, so powerful, so dramatic, that they take possession of the organism and compel it to become the means of their manifestation. In mediumistic trance the same thing happens. There may be suggestion from outside, or there may not, but in the depth of the medium's mind images are formed which speak and act through the entranced person, making use in doing so of the marvellous stores of memory and knowledge which the inner mind has at command, and sorely puzzling the spectators at times, as to whether the performance is merely histrionic or whether by chance it indicates a *bona fide* communication from the dead.[70]

This energetic dramatic quality of the image-forming faculty is tremendously important. It has not been enough insisted upon; and it has been greatly misunderstood and misrepresented. It is, as I say, a root-property of creation. It is seen everywhere in the healthy activity of the human mind, in its delight in romance and imagination, in the play of children, the stage, literature, art, scientific invention—the sheer joy of creation, going on everywhere and always. Lay the conscious and controlling and selective power of the upper mind at rest, in the trance-condition, and you have in the deeps of the subliminal self this primal creative power exposed. Offer to it the lightest suggestion, and there springs forth from that abyss a figure corresponding, or a dozen figures, or a whole procession! The mere delight of creation calls them forth. Could anything be more wonderful? What a strange glimpse it gives us of the possibilities of Creation.

Some people seem to be quite shocked at the idea that this subliminal mind, or whatever it is that possesses these marvellous powers, should act these parts, and lend itself to unsubstantial and quasi-fraudulent representations. But why accuse of deception? It is a game—the great game we are all of us playing—the whole Creation romancing away; with endless inexhaustible fertility throwing out images, ideas, new shapes and forms forever. Those forms which hold their own, which substantiate themselves, which fill a place, fulfil a need—they win their way into the actual world and become the originals of the plants, the animals, human beings, works of art, and so forth, which we know. Those which cannot hold their own pass back again into the unseen. In the far depths of the entranced medium's mind we see this abysmal process going on—this fountain-like production of images taking place—the very beginnings of creation. It is the sheer joy of manifestation. As one gives a musician a mere hint or clue—a theme of three or four notes—and immediately he improvises a spirited piece of music; so is it with the hypnotized person or with the medium. One gives him a suggestion and he immediately creates the figures according. And so it is for us, to direct this wonderful power, even in ourselves—not to call it fraudulent, but to make use of it for splendid ends.

Doubtless it can be used for unworthy ends. It is easy to understand that the mediumistic person, finding this wonderful dramatic and creative faculty within himself or herself, is sometimes tempted to turn it to personal advantage; and succumbs to the temptation. The dramatic habit catches hold of the waking self, and renders the person tricky and unreliable.[71] But below it all is creation, and the instinct of creation—the power that gives to airy nothing a local habitation, the genius of the dramatist, of the artist, of the inventor, and the *very source of the visible and tangible world.*

For from the Under-self—as exposed in the state of trance, or in extreme languor and exhaustion of the body, or in the moment of death, or in dreams, or even in profound reverie—proceed (strange as it may seem) Voices and Visions and Forms, things audible and visible and tangible, things anyhow which are competent to impress the senses of spectators so vividly as to be for the moment indistinguishable from the phenomena, audible, visible and tangible, of our actual world. Amazing as are the materializations connected with mediums—the figures which appear, which speak, which touch and are touched, the faces, the supernumerary feet and hands, the sounds, the lights, the movements of objects—all in some way connected with the medium's presence—these phenomena are now far too well established and confirmed by careful and scientific observation to admit (in the mass) of any reasonable doubt.[72] And similarly with the wraiths, or phantoms which are projected from dying or lately dead persons, the evidence for them in general is much too abundant and well attested to allow of disbelief.[73] What an extraordinary story, for instance, is that given by Sir Oliver Lodge in his *Survival of Man* (p.)—of a workman who having drunk poison by mistake, appeared in the moment of death, with blue and blotched face to his employer, to whom he was greatly attached, and told him not to be deceived by the rumor that he (the workman) had committed suicide! Yet the story is fully and authoritatively given in the *Proceedings of the Society for Psychical Research*, vol. iii. p. 97, and cannot well be set aside. But if such things happen in the hour of death, so do they also happen in the dream-state.[74] The dreamer has a vivid dream of visiting a certain person, and is accordingly and at that time, seen by that person. And in the state of reverie the same. It is at times sufficient to think profoundly of any one, or to let one's inner self go out toward that person in order to cause an image of oneself to be seen by him.

It will of course be said, and often is said, that those phenomena are only hallucinations, and have no objective existence. But the sufficient answer to that is that the things also of our actual world are hallucinations in their degree, and certainly have no full objective existence. The daffodil in my garden is an hallucination in that degree that with the smallest transposition of my senses, its color, its scent, and even its form might be quite altered. What we call its objectivity rests on the permanence of its relations—on its continued appearance in one spot, its visibility to different people at one time, or to one person at different times, and so forth. But if that is the definition of objectivity, it is obvious that the forms which have been seen over and over again, and under strict test-conditions, in connection with certain mediums, have had in their degree an objective existence.

In America, in connection with Kate Fox (one of the earliest and most spontaneous and natural of modern mediums), a certain Mr. Livermore—a thoroughly capable business man of New York—came into communication as it seemed with his deceased wife. She appeared to him—not in one house only, but in several houses—over and over again; sometimes only the head, sometimes the whole figure; her appearance was accompanied by inexplicable sounds and lights; she communicated sometimes by raps, sometimes by visibly writing on blank cards brought for the purpose; and these phenomena extended over a period of six years and recorded sittings, and at many of the sittings were corroborated by independent witnesses.[75] It is difficult to imagine hallucinations or deceit maintained under such circumstances.

In England (in connection with the medium Florence Cook) the figure "Katie King" appeared to Sir William Crookes a great number of times during three years (1–84) and was studied by him and Mr. C. F. Varley, F.R.S., with the greatest scientific care. Her apparition often spoke to those present, was touched by, and touched them, wrote, or played with the children. It often came outside the cabinet, and three times was seen by those present simultaneously with, and by the side of, the entranced medium. The figure was taller than the medium and different in feature;

Crookes observed its pulse and found it making 75 beats a minute to the medium's 90, and so forth.[76]

Professor Richet, the French scientist, examined with great care the phantasm "Beni Boa," which appeared to him some twenty times in connection with the Algerian medium Aisha; he obtained several photographs of it, and observed its pulse, its respiration, and so forth.[77] Lombroso, the author of many scientific works, and a man who to begin with was a complete sceptic on these matters, assures us that at the sittings of Eusapia Paladino he saw his own mother (long dead) a great number of times, and that she repeatedly kissed him.[78] In connection with Mme. D'Espérance[79] the girlish figure of "Yolanda" appeared and disappeared very frequently during a period of ten years, and was well known to frequenters of her circle; and in 6 a committee formed by some twenty-five high officials and well-known persons in Norway publicly attested the repeated appearance at her seances of a very beautiful female figure who glided among the sitters, grasped their hands, gave them messages, and so forth, and disappeared before their eyes in a misty cloud.[80] Such evidence of the objectivity of seance figures could be rather indefinitely multiplied. But the same may be said, though perhaps less conclusively, of various ghosts and other manifestations, whose relations to certain persons or places or houses seem quite definite and well established—and not unfrequently steadily recurrent under the same conditions.[81]

Without going into the vexed question of whether these and the like manifestations are merely products or inventions of the trance-mind of the medium or other person concerned, or whether some at least of them are the work or evidence of separate 'spirits'—leaving that question open for the present—we may still say that all these things are actual creations—creations of the hidden self of Man in some form or other; not so assured, certainly, and not so permanent as the well-known shapes of outer Nature; abortive creations, if you like, which come a little way forward into manifestation, and then retreat again; but still creations in the same sense as those more established ones; and wonderfully revealing to us the secret of the generation and birth of all the visible world.

That we should have, all of us, this magic source somewhere buried within—this Aladdin's lamp, this vase of the Djinns, this Pandora box of evil as well as of good, is indeed astounding; and must cause us, when we have once fully realized the fact, to envisage life quite differently from what we have ever done before. It must cause us to feel that our very ordinary and daily self—which we know so well (and which sometimes we even get a little tired of) is only a fraction, only a flag and a signal, of that great Presence which we really are, that great Mass-man who lies unexplored behind the very visible and actual. Difficult or impossible as this being may be to define, enormously complex as it probably is, and far-reaching, and hard to gauge, yet we see that it is *there*, undeniably there—a being that apparently includes far extremes of faculty and character, running parallel to the conscious self from low to high levels,[82] having in its range of manifestation the most primitive desires and passions, and the highest feats of intellect and enthusiasm; and while at times capable of accepting the most frivolous suggestions and of behaving in a humorous or merely capricious and irresponsible manner, at other times capable, as we have seen, of taking most serious command and control of the whole physical organism, and as far as the spiritual organism is concerned, of rising to the greatest heights of prophecy and inspiration.[83]

I say, then, that we must include in this problem of survival both the ordinary upper and conscious self and the deep-lying subjective and subconscious (or superconscious) being. Just as the organizing power of the Body includes the Cerebro-spinal system of nerves on the one hand, and the Great-Sympathetic system on the other, so the organism of the soul includes the supraliminal and subliminal portions. The two must be taken together, and either alone could only represent a fraction of the real person. The exact relation of these two selves to each other is a matter which can only become clear with long time and study of this difficult subject. It may be that the subliminal self is destined to become conscious in our ordinary sense of the word. It may be, on the other hand, that the conscious self is destined to rise into the much wider consciousness of the subjective being. There is a great deal to suggest that the supraliminal self is only the front as it were of the great wave of life; and that the brain consciousness is only a very special instrument for dealing with the surroundings and conditions of our terrestrial existence—an instrument which will surrender much of its value at death and on mergence with the larger and differently constituted consciousness which underruns and sustains it. That the two selves are in constant communication with each other, and that they are both intelligent in some sense, is obvious from the facts of *suggestion*, by which often the lightest whisper so to speak from the upper is understood and attended to by the under self; while, on the other hand, the under-self communicates with the upper, sometimes by inner Voices heard and Visions seen, sometimes by automatic actions, as in dream- or trance-writing, sometimes even by Sounds and Apparitions so powerful as to *appear* at least external.

So we cannot but think that the question of survival may ultimately resolve itself very much into the question of the more complete and effectual understanding between these different portions of the self. When they come into clear relation with each other, when the unit-man and the Mass-man merge into a perfect understanding and harmony, when they both become conscious of their affiliation to the great Self of the universe, then the problem will be solved—or we may perhaps say, the problem will cease to exist

NOTE TO CHAPTER VIII

ON TRANCE-PHENOMENA

It may seem rash or unbalanced to dwell, in the preceding chapters, on trance and mediumistic phenomena as much as I have done, considering that they are in some sense abnormal—that is, they are unusual, and comparatively few people have an opportunity of verifying them; also they may (it is said) be abnormal in the sense of being the products of conditions so special or even so morbid that conclusions drawn from them can have no general importance or value.

There is a certain fashion in such matters, and with large sections of the public and during a long period it has no doubt been the habit simply to dismiss all consideration of this subject, as for one reason or another unadvisable. But now these phenomena in general (or enough of them to constitute a solid body of observation) are so thoroughly corroborated that it would be mere affectation to pass them by; and the best science nowadays refuses to ignore exceptional happenings on account of their exceptionality—recognizing that these very happenings often afford the key to the explanation of more common events.

The phenomena connected with mediums and seances have been so amazing and unexpected that they have often produced a kind of fear and dismay. The religious people have been terrified at the prospect of having to acknowledge miracles not connected with the Church; or of having to confess to the resurrection of John Smith as well as of Jesus Christ. The scientific folk (in many or most quarters) being always just on the point of completing their pet scheme of the universe—whatever it may happen to be at the time—have naturally been in no mood to admit new facts which would totally disarrange their systems; and have, therefore, with a few brilliant exceptions, consistently closed their eyes or looked another way. And the general public, not without reason, has feared to embark on a subject which might easily float it away from the dry land of practical life, into one knows not what sea of doubt or even delusion.

But these difficulties attend at all times the introduction of a new subject—or at least of one which is new to the generation concerned; and can of course not be allowed to interfere with the candid and impartial examination of the subject, or with the assimilation, as far as feasible, of its message. It should certainly, I think, be admitted that there are dangers attending the new science—or rather attending the hasty and careless investigation of it—just as there are attending any other science. There is no doubt that the phenomena connected with it are so astounding that they in some cases unhinge people's minds, or at least for the time upset them; and what we have already said once or twice of the frequent bodily exhaustion of the Medium, not to mention the occasional exhaustion of the sitters, must convince us that the greatest care should be exercised in connection with trance-conditions, and that the whole subject should be studied with a view to discovering its proper and best handling. It is clear—whatever view is taken of the process—that a certain disintegration of the organism, and even of the personality of the medium, is liable to occur, one portion of the organism acting in a manner and under influences foreign to another portion, and that such disintegration oft repeated or long continued may be liable to produce a permanent degeneration of physique or even possibly demoralization of character. If there is a danger in this direction—and the extent of the danger should certainly be gauged—equally certainly it ought to be minimized or averted by the proper conditions. On the other hand, while noting this danger, we should not leave out of mind that some evidence points in the other direction—namely, to the favorable effects and influences of trance when rightly conducted.[84] We may also in this connection allude to the changed attitude of the general mind to-day toward Hypnotism—a subject allied to that which we are considering. Fifty years ago the word had a sinister sound, and hypnotism and mesmerism were thought to be inventions of the devil and agencies of all evil. To-day they are recognized as a great power for good, and in at least two hospitals (in France) as the main instrument of healing. Naturally, when people are ignorant of a subject, or only in the first stages of knowledge with regard to it, they mishandle and misunderstand it. It may well happen therefore that with better understanding of mediumship and trance-conditions, some of their drawbacks or less favorable aspects may pass out of sight.

Mediums and trance-phenomena—prophecy, second sight, speaking in strange tongues, the appearance of flames and lights, and of figures apparently from the dead—are things that have been known all down history, and recognized almost as a matter of course, both among quite primitive peoples like the Kaffirs, or the Aleuts or the Mongolians, or among the more cultured like the Greeks, the Romans, the Hindus, Chinese, and so forth. The Bible teems with references to wizards and "necromancers" (note the meaning of the word); and the story of the Witch of Endor gives us a penetrating glimpse into what was evidently a common practice of "consultation." These phenomena have never been so common as to break up and disorganize the routine of ordinary life, yet they have always been there, and recognized, as on the fringe or borderland—in somewhat the same way as the knowledge or recognition of Death does not interfere with daily life or prevent us making engagements; though we know it *may* do so at any time. And beyond any direct uses that trance-communication and manifestations may have now, or may have had in the past (a matter on which no doubt there is a good deal of difference of opinion), we may fairly suppose that as examples of real things and of a real world lying just outside the sphere of our ordinary and actual experience they may be of immense value—both as delivering us from a cramped and petty belief that we have already fathomed the possibilities of the universe, and as giving us just a hint and a glimpse of directions in which we may fairly look for the future. That we should for the present be limited for the most part to a definite sphere of activity, or to a definite region of creation, seems only natural. "One world, please, at a time!" said Thoreau when on his deathbed he was plagued by some pious person about the future life; and if *we* in our daily life were entangled in the manifestations of two very different planes of existence it might be greatly baffling. At the same time, the occasional hint or message from another plane may be of the greatest help.

Condensations and manifestations (as of beings from such other plane) may be abnormal at present. They may be rare, they may occur under unexpected and even unhealthy conditions, they may cause dislocations of mind and of morals, they may be confused and confusing. All these things we should indeed in some degree *expect*; and yet it may not follow that these objections will continue. It is quite possible that in the future they will disappear. As I have had occasion to say many times, every new movement or manifestation of human activity, when unfamiliar to people's minds, is sure to be misrepresented and misunderstood. It appears in humble guise, without backing or patronage, forcing its way to light in the most unlikely places, "to the Jews a stumbling-block, to the Greeks foolishness," often distorted and out of shape owing to its very birth-struggles, and for the very same reason diffident at first and uncertain of its own mission. Possibly a time is coming when Mediumship, instead of being left over (as not unfrequently now) to quite ignorant and uncultured specimens of humanity, and being exercised in haphazard, careless fashion, or for monetary gain, or personal vanity, will be looked upon as a sacred and responsible office, worthy of and requiring considerable preparation and instruction, demanding the respect of the public, yet thoroughly criticized, both in method and result, by intelligent examination and logic. Possibly a time is coming when messages and manifestations from another plane than that of our daily life will come to us under the most obviously healthy and sane conditions, and will be fully recognized as having value and even, in their way, authority.

For the present—allowing (as I do) the absolute genuineness of a great body of "spiritualistic" phenomena—there still is (owing to various causes already indicated) considerable doubt as to *who* or *what* the manifesting beings or forces are. I suppose the main theories on the subject may be gathered under the following heads: that the manifesting powers are (1) Images, more or less unconsciously projected from the Medium's own mind; or, in case of raps, and so forth, emissions of force from the medium's body; (2) that they are the same projected from the minds or bodies of other persons present; (3) that they are independent Beings, making *use* of the medium's or other person's organism for the purpose of expression; or (4) that there is a blending of these actions.

I think everyone who has studied the matter practically admits the first explanation in some degree; most people perhaps allow the second and fourth; but a good many—though not all—exclude the third. With regard, however, to this last theory (that there really are occasional messages or manifestations from the dead—or from "the other side") there certainly seems to be a very considerable residuum of evidence which, though not absolutely conclusive, is favorable to it; and there certainly are a considerable number of eminent and responsible men—like Myers, Lodge, Lombroso, and others—who, though not dogmatic, profess themselves inclined to accept the theory, on the evidence so far available. For myself—having so little personal and direct experience in this field—I do not feel in a position to form a definite opinion, and am content to leave the evidence to accumulate.

CHAPTER IX

SURVIVAL OF THE SELF

IN the last chapter we pointed out that for any adequate understanding of the subject before us the self must be taken to include the more obscure and subconscious portion of the mind, as well as the specially conscious portion with which we are most familiar. There is a constant interaction and flow taking place between the two parts, and to draw a strict line dividing them would be impossible. Indeed it would rather appear that growth comes largely by their blending and throwing light on each other. We also brought forward some considerations to show the nature of the underlying or subconscious self—its immense extent, the swiftness of its perceptions, and so forth. If then, to continue our argument, there should come a time (in death) when the outer and more obvious ego merges, or at least comes into closer relation, with the under-self, it would seem likely that the surviving consciousness would be greatly changed from its present form, and would take on something of the instantaneous wide-reaching character of what has been called the Cosmic Consciousness. And this is a conclusion much to be expected, and surely also much to be desired. However one may envisage the matter, it hardly seems possible to imagine an after-death consciousness quite on the same plane as our present consciousness. (This, too—one may say in passing—probably explains the difficulty we experience in holding direct communication with the dead—the same sort of difficulty, in fact, that the outer mind during life has in directly reaching the inner mind.) Myers[85] speaks of our supraliminal life as merely a special phase of our whole personality, and suggests that there are good reasons for thinking that there is a relation—"obscure but indisputable—between the subliminal and the surviving self." Under these circumstances it would seem natural to inquire what definite reasons there may be for thinking that the subliminal self survives; and I shall occupy this chapter largely with that question.

(1) In the first place, from the observed process of the generation and growth of the body from a microscopic origin, we have already argued (chapter vii.) the probability of the pre-existence in a sub-atomic or fourth-dimensional state of the being which is manifested in the body, and therefore the probability of the continuance of that being after the dissolution of the body. And this argument must include the Under-self, which is responsible for so much of the organization and growth and sustentation of the body, as well as the Upper; and may well lead us to

infer that both upper and under selves continue after death—only conjoined in some way, and with some added experience gained during life.

(2) In the second place, we are struck by the fact that continuous Memory—which we decided to be the very necessary condition of survival—is just the thing which is so strong in the subjective being and so characteristic of it. The huge stores of memory—and of quite *personal and individual* memory—which this being has at command, their long dormancy and their extraordinary resurgence at times when conditions call them forth, are a marvel to the investigator, and make us feel that it is hardly probable that they are all swept away at death. Even if dormant *at* the time of death, it seems not unlikely that here again later conditions may awake them once more to life.

But (3), we have a great deal of evidence to show that, as a matter of fact, the underlying self is especially *active* at the moment of death. The whole phenomenon of 'wraiths'—now in the mass so amply proved[86]—the projection of phantasms sometimes to an immense distance,[87] by persons *in articulo mortis*—goes to show its intense energy and *vitality* (if one may use the word) at that moment. And the vivid resurgences of memory at the same moment (or in any hour of danger) point in the same direction. T. J. Hudson, and others, insist that the subjective mind *never sleeps*—that whatever drowsiness, or faintness, or languor may overpower the upper or self-conscious mind, the under mind is still acutely awake and operant, and if this is (as it appears) true with regard to sleep, it may well also be so even with regard to death.

Again (4), the Telæsthetic faculty of the under-self (I mean during life)—its power of clairvoyantly perceiving things and events at a distance, even in minutest details—is a very wonderful fact—a fact that is amply established, and one that must give us pause. Here are vision and perception at work without eyes or ears, or any of the usual bodily end-organs[88]—and acting in such a way as to suggest or practically to prove that the soul has other channels or instruments of perception than those connected with the well-known outer body. Every one has heard of cases of this kind. They are common on the borderland of sleep, or in dreams, and—what especially appeals to us here—they are very common in the hour of death. If the soul (as is evidently the case) can perceive without the intermediation of mortal eye or ear; then—though we may conclude that these special organs have been fashioned or developed for special terrene use—we may also conclude that, without them, it would still continue to exercise perception, developing sight and hearing and other faculties along lines with which at present we are but slightly acquainted. These faculties spring inevitably deep down out of ourselves, and will recur again doubtless wherever we are.... "Were your eyes destroyed, still the faculty of sight were not destroyed; out of the same roots again as before would another optic apparatus spring."[89]

And the same may be said, (5), about the telepathic faculty—that is, the power (not of perceiving, but) of *sending* impressions or messages to a distance. This power which the under-self has of communicating with the under-selves of other persons, and often at a great distance, is one of the best-established facts in the new psychology; and again, it is very pregnant with inference. It shows us the soul acting vividly along certain lines independent as far as we can see of the known body, certainly along lines independent of the known organs of expression. It compels us to conclude a possible and even probable activity quite apart from that body. With this telepathic power, or as an extension of it, may be classed the image-projecting faculty, which we have already seen to be peculiarly active in death. And it may be appropriate here to notice that in quite a number of the cases of wraiths or phantasms projected (in forty cases out of three hundred and sixteen as given by Edmund Gurney in *Proceedings S.P.R.* vol. v. p.) the apparition was seen after the death had occurred—though within twenty-four hours after. This may directly indicate an after-death activity of the person who projected the image, or it *may* merely indicate a relay of the telepathic impression on its way, or in the subconscious mind of the recipient, previous to emerging in the latter's *conscious* mind.[90]

All these things are strongly indicative. They do not give the impression that at death the underlying self is in the act of perishing. On the contrary, they point to its continuance, and if anything *increased* activity; while at the same time the strongly *personal* character of many of the phenomena referred to—the wonderfully distinct personal memories, the very personal images or phantasms projected, the telepathic appeal to nearest and dearest friends—all suggest that the continuing activity does not merely tail off into an abstract life-force or vague stream of tendency, but is of a distinctly personal or individual character.

There is another consideration, (6), on which I may dwell for a moment here. The passion of Love, whether considered in its physical or in its psychical and emotional aspects, is notably a matter of the subjective or subliminal life. The little self-conscious, logical, argumentative personality is completely routed by this passion, which seems to spring from the great depths of being with Titanic force, full-armed in its own convictions, and overturning all established orders and conventions. It surely must give us a deep insight into the nature of that hidden self from which it springs. Yet nothing is more noticeable about the passion than its recklessness of mortal life—nothing more noticeable than its willingness to sacrifice all worldly prospects and the body itself in the pursuit of its ends. Even the most physical love, as we have said already (chapter vi.), has a strange relation to Death, and often slays the very object of its desire:—

> "For each man kills the thing he loves,
>
> Though each man does not die."

While the more emotional form of the passion almost rejoices in its contempt of life and its willingness to face dangers and death for the sake of the beloved. It says as plain as words:—"I can fulfil myself and my purposes all right, even without this mortal part which you hold so dear"; and unless we think that the hidden being who thus speaks is a perfect fool, we must conclude that it is *aware* of a life surpassing that of the body.

Such a continuing life we no doubt have evidence of, and indeed commonly admit to exist, in the Race-life; and as a first approximation it seems natural and obvious to interpret the underlying or subliminal self as being simply the Race-self. In the case of the lower and less developed forms of creation, perhaps this is the wisest thing to do. In default of more detailed and perfect knowledge, we may easily assume that in a shoal of several million herrings or in a 'culture' of several billion microbes the underlying self of each particular herring or microbe is practically identical with the self of the race concerned. But in the case of man and some of the higher animals it is not so easy to do this. We find a strongly individual element in his subconscious mind, which must also be accounted for. I have already alluded to the stores of individual memory which this mind retains, thus differentiating it from others; and I have alluded to the intensely individual phantasms which it projects. And now again we are brought face to face with the greatly individual character of its love-passion. However much the love-passion may be symbolical of the life of the race, and deeply implicated in the same (and both of these it certainly is), still—except in its lower forms—there is nothing vague and general and undifferentiated about that passion; on the contrary, it is most strongly personal and sharply outlined. Why is it that out of the hundred thousand people that a man may meet only *one* will arouse this tremendous response? Why is it that every great love in its depth seems different from every other? Do not these things suggest a profound difference of outline in the subconscious beings themselves from whom these loves proceed? These beings are manifestations and organic expressions of the Race—yes. But they are also deeply individual and different—each one from the other.

And here we seem to come upon the first emergence of the solution of the problem before us. The self of which we are in search *has*—especially through its subconscious part—a vast continuing life, affiliated to the life of the race and beyond that to the cosmic life of the All; but it also has a strongly individual outline and character. Nursed in the womb of the Race during countless ages, like a babe within its mother, passing through numberless reincarnations in a kind of collective way, and in more or less unconsciousness of its supreme and separate destiny, it at last in Man attains to the clear sense of individuality, and (through much suffering) is set free to an independent existence; being finally exhaled from earth-mortality into a cosmic life under other conditions of space and time than ours.

Difficult as this conception of a continued individual existence may be to hold to in view of the terrible and external flux of general Nature, and difficult as it may be to understand in all detail; yet, as I say, it is Love which compels us to the insight of its truth. It is Love which has the clear conception of the uniqueness of the beloved, it is love which positively refuses to believe in her (or his) annihilation, it is love alone which in the hour of loss can face the awful midnight sky, and dare to sing:—

"Sleep sweetly, tender heart, in peace,

Sleep, holy Spirit, blessed soul!

While the stars burn, the moons increase,

And the great ages onward roll."

And it is in the meeting of lovers that the heavens open, allowing them to see—if only for a moment—the eternities to which they both belong.

There are no doubt other considerations—I mean those connected with mediumistic and so-called spiritualistic phenomena—which point toward the conclusion of an individual survival of some kind after death; but although this kind of evidence is likely to prove in the end of immense value, it is possible that the time has not yet quite come when it can be completely substantiated, tabulated, and effectively utilized; at any rate I do not feel myself in a position to so deal with it. It has also to be said that a great deal of this evidence (relating to actual communications from the dead) is necessarily of so very personal a character that it can only appeal to the individual persons concerned, and however convincing it may be to them does naturally not carry the same conviction to the world at large. I shall therefore for the present pass these considerations by, and, on the strength of the arguments already brought forward, assume the general truth of man's survival.

The course of the argument has been somewhat as follows. In the first place, we have urged the enormous possibilities (disclosed by modern investigation) of other life than that which we know—thus enlarging the bounds of the likely, and weakening the argument from improbability. In the second place, we have pointed out that continuance of *memory* seems the best test of survival; that even in our law courts (as in a Tichborne case) it is not so much the facts of feature and form as the facts of memory which are relied on to prove identity. Thirdly, we have argued that not only the supraliminal but also the subliminal self must be considered in this matter, and that probably the surviving self will arise from a harmony or conjunction between these two. Fourthly, we have shown that in respect of memory and many other matters the subliminal self shows a quite remarkable activity even in the hour of bodily death—which does not certainly suggest its decease and cessation from existence. Fifthly, we have seen that all through life the soul has faculties (of clairvoyance, transposition of senses, and so forth) which point to its independence of the material body. Sixthly, that through *love* it reaches a deep conviction of its own duration beyond the life of the body. And, seventhly, we have suggested that it is largely through the supraliminal and self-conscious life that the sense of identity and individuality is educed and finally established.

Proceeding, then, further along these lines, the next and obvious question which arises is, In what sort of body is this continuing life manifested? That it must be manifested in some sort of body is, I think, clear. If we had only arrived at the conclusion that at death the human being merged in the All-soul, or became an indistinguishable portion of the 'Happy Mass'—that his individual memory flowed out into the great ocean of the world-memory and became lost in it, and that his power of individual action or perception passed away in like manner—why then the question of a continuing body could not well arise, or at farthest stretch such body could only be thought of as something indistinguishable from the entire universe. But if there is any truth in the idea of an individual survival, then it seems clear that there must be some kind of *form*, to mark the bounds of the individual, and to give outline to his relations to other individuals—whether those relations be active and invasive or passive and receptive; there must be some surface of resistance and separation.

With this question I shall deal in the next chapter. Before, however, going into any definite theory of this 'soul-body,' it may be useful to dwell for a moment on general considerations. In the first place, it is clear that if the individual survives, he does not do so in any fixed and unchanging form. The form of the individual is not fixed in this earth-life; nor can we expect or wish it to be so in any other life. As long as there is a continuous stream of experience and memory, going on from this life to another life, and from that perchance to others—that is all we can expect to find. There may, indeed, be a fixed and transcendent Individuality, an aspect of the Universal, at the root of all these experiences, but with that we are hardly concerned at this moment—only with the stream of personal manifestations which proceed from it—everchanging yet linked together from hour to hour. In the second place, though we have dwelt upon and emphasized the idea of separateness and differentiation, in the surviving self, in contra-distinction to the idea of fusion in a formless aggregate, yet it is clear here too that the common life and bonds must hold individuals together, just as much as, if not more than, in the earth-life. The salient facts of telepathy, sympathy, clairvoyance, and so forth convince us that souls, freed to some extent from their grosser present envelopes, will react upon each other in the future, or in that farther world, more swiftly and more intimately than they do now. And as they progress from stage to stage, developing individualities and differences always on a grander and grander scale, so they will also develop through love their organic union with each other. It seems possible, indeed, that growth will largely take place *through* love-fusion; till at length, rising into the highest ranges of combined Individuality and Universality, the transformed consciousness of each soul will take on its true quality—"that of space itself—which is at rest everywhere."

CHAPTER X

THE INNER OR SPIRITUAL BODY

IN order to form a conception of what kind of body the surviving Self may have, it seems best for the moment to go back to the genesis of our present body. We saw (chapter vii.) that we were compelled to suppose, even in the first germ of our actual body an intelligent form of some kind at work, which while gathering up and representing race-memories of the past, presided over and directed their rehabilitation in the present, thus building up the present body according to a certain pattern—(though subject of course to modification by outer difficulties and obstacles). From the very first, the exceeding complexity and delicacy of the movements within the germ-cells, combined with the decisiveness of their divisions and differentiations, and the perfection and adaptation of the bodily structures and organs ultimately produced, all point in the suggested direction.[91] At the same time, we were compelled to conclude that this form, whose first manifestations in the tiny germ-cell evidently originate from quite ultra-microscopic movements, was itself invisible, invisible through belonging either to an ultra-microscopic world, or to a world of a fourth-dimensional or other order of existence. I think, therefore, that for the present we may accept that conclusion, and fairly suppose that some such invisible form underlies the genesis of each of our bodies.

But at the same time the conclusion of invisibility must not be supposed to carry with it the conclusion of immateriality. Quite the contrary. A creature living in the two-dimensional world formed by the water-film on the surface of a pond might have no conception of the water-world below or the air-world above—both of which might be quite invisible to it; all the same a fish or a bird breaking through the surface would instantly cause some very powerful and very material phenomena there! And again, though atoms and electrons individually may be quite invisible, it is only a question of their number and the force of their electric charges, as to how far they intrude upon what we call the material world. Also, we must remember that invisibility or imperceptibility does not by any means imply non-occupation of space. On the contrary again. For four-dimensional existence carries with it an occupation of space which is quite miraculous to us—as, for instance, the power of appearing in two places at the same time; while a number of ultra-microscopic atoms, by their electrostatic attractions and repulsions, may maintain definite relations of distance from each other, and may altogether constitute a cloud of considerable size and complex organization—quite imperceptible as a rule, yet occupying a definite area and fully capable of affecting material things.

It may be a question, then, whether it is not some such invisible cloud—perhaps of quite human size and measurement—which at conception begins to enter the fertilized germ-cell, stimulating it to division, and penetrating further and further into the newly-formed body-cells, as by thousands and millions they divide and multiply to form the growing organism. Whatever it is, it is something of infinitely subtle organization and constitution, representing the inmost vitality of the body, and not that inmost vitality in a merely general sense, but the vitality of every portion and section of the body. It establishes itself within the gross body (or it builds that body round itself) and becomes the organizer and provider of its life; maintains its form and structure during life, fortifies it against change and disease, and wards off as long as it can the arrival of death.

What, then, of Death? Why, granted so much as we have supposed, it seems easy to suppose that at death this inner body passes away again. It just leaves the gross body behind and passes out of it. For a fourth-dimensional being this must be easy to do! But not to presume too much on other-dimensional conditions, if we only assume the inner body to be such a cloud of atoms or electrons as already mentioned, the passage of such atoms through the tissues of the gross body would be entirely in accordance with the well-known facts of *osmose* and the diffusion of liquids and gases, and would present no exceptional or impossible problem. Through cell-walls and muscular and other tissues such atoms would pass, conceivably maintaining still their relative 'form' and organization with regard to each other, and forming a cloud similar to that which entered the germ and other cells at conception (though of course so far modified by the life-experience), and leaving now the gross body devitalized, and doomed to slow corruption and to serve only as material for lower forms.

One would not, of course, venture on conjectures so speculative as the above, if it were not that long tradition and history, and even modern experience, so singularly confirm or favor their general truth. The conception of a cloud-like ghost—sometimes visible, sometimes invisible[92]—leaving the body at death, roaming through the fields of Hades or some hidden world, and from time to time revisiting the glimpses of the moon and the gaze of wondering mortals—penetrates all literature and tradition. Among all primitive peoples it seems to be accepted as a matter of course; it informs the legends and the drama and the philosophies of the more cultivated; it claims detailed historical instances and proofs[93] (as in the case of Field-marshal von Grumbkoff, to whom the wraith of King Frederick Augustus announced his own death—which had just occurred; or in the case of the poet Petrarch, to whom Bishop Colonna made a similar announcement); and in modern times it has met with extraordinary and in many quarters quite unexpected confirmation at the hands of scientific investigation.

To this evidence of general probability that at death a vital and subtle yet substantial inner body is withdrawn from every part and portion of the gross body, we may add the evidence, such as it is, from actual *sensation* and *experience*. In the hour of death and in allied physical changes sensations are experienced corresponding to such a conclusion. Though necessarily there is little quite direct evidence, for the actual moment of death, yet in the just preceding stage, of extreme weakness, the sensation of depletion in every part of the body, and of withdrawal, as of a hand being drawn out of a glove, is very noticeable. (And it may be remarked that clairvoyants not unfrequently observe, at death itself, a luminous cloud of the general outline and shape of the dying person being slowly distilled, head first, from his or her head.) Furthermore, in the state of *ecstasy*—which is closely allied to death—the same sensation of withdrawal is experienced. The person seems to himself to stand outside and a little beyond his own body—and doubtless this experience is denoted in the very etymology of the word. In trance the same: the medium experiences the extreme of exhaustion while some portion of her vital being is functioning (as it appears) outside. Under anæsthetics it is a common experience to dream that one has left the body and is flying through space. (See *The Art of Creation*, p. 18.) And again, in the case of love—whose close relation to death we have several times already noted—whether it be in the strain of emotional desire or the stress of the physical orgasm this 'hand from the glove' sensation is often most acute and seems to suggest that every portion of the body is contributing its part to the process in hand; which indeed in this case of love may very fairly be supposed to consist in a transfer of the cloud-like organism (or a large part of it) to the other person concerned.

There are cases, too, where in a kind of dream-consciousness the sensation of the self passing out through walls and other obstacles is so powerful as to leave an impress on the mind ever after. Such is the case already alluded to (chapter viii. p. , *supra*) from *Footfalls on the Boundary of Another World*, where a lady half waking from sleep "felt herself carried to the wall of her room, with a feeling that it must arrest her further progress. But no; she seemed to pass through it into the open air. Outside the house was a tree; and this also she appeared to traverse as if it interposed no obstacle." She thus passed to the house of a lady friend, held a conversation with her, and in her dream returned. But afterward the friend reported that she had *seen* the apparition that night and conversed with it. Similarly a young friend of mine, dreaming one night that his mother (in the same house) was ill, was intensely conscious of dashing—not along corridors and through doorways but *through the partition walls of two rooms*—into the chamber where his mother slept, when finding her all right he returned; and the experience was so vivid that it remained with him for days afterward.

Taking all these considerations together, we may say that there is a strong general probability in favor of the proposition put forward. And it is interesting and important to find that at this juncture modern science is coming out from her old haunts and beginning seriously to tackle a question which she has hitherto for the most part evaded or ignored. The whole of the psychology and even physiology of Death have (as I have previously remarked) been sadly neglected; but now and of late quite a number of books on this subject have been published,[94] and a good deal of scientific activity is moving in that direction.

Professor Fournier d'Albe, in his book *New Light on Immortality*,[95] has made some very interesting suggestions—which though they may not as yet be accounted more than suggestions, seem to be in the right direction, and certainly acquire some authority from his intimate command of the modern discoveries in Physics as well as in the field of Psychical Research. His view is that every one of the twenty-five thousand million million cells which constitute say the human body has probably some 'centrosome' or other vital point within it, which is in fact the governing and organizing power of that cell. Such point or collection of points, though 'material,' may likely weigh only a ten-thousandth part of the cell-weight. Hence if this 'soul' was abstracted from each cell, the total weight of the twenty-five thousand billion souls resulting would be only a ten-thousandth part of the body weight, or about a fifth of an ounce! But these soul-fragments or *psychomeres* as he calls them, would together make up the total soul of the man, and—as already explained—might not only by their negative and positive charges maintain certain spatial relations and organization with regard to each other, but would, owing to their extreme minuteness, easily pass through the tissues and liberate themselves from the gross body. Thus a human soul, weighing a fraction only of an ounce, but of like shape and size to the human body, and of intense vitality and subtlety, might disengage itself at death, to begin a fresh career and to enter into a new life—leaving the existing body to fall to ruin and decay. Further, Professor Fournier d'Albe, greatly bold in speculation, surmises that such a spiritual body, discharging the atmosphere from its interior frame, might quite naturally rise in the air till it attained its position of equilibrium at a great height up—say in a region 35–80 miles over the earth, which would thus become the (first) abode of the departed.

Whatever may be said about the details of this theory, and whatever difficulties they may present, the main outlines—as I have already indicated—seem quite feasible and probable, and in line with world-old belief and tradition. And certain details (which we shall return to again) are powerfully corroborated by modern observation.

Meanwhile it is interesting to find, in corroboration of the general theory, that some experiments lately carried out, in weighing the body before and after death, have apparently yielded the result of a decided loss of weight at or very shortly after, the moment of Death. Dr. Duncan M'Dougall, experimenting with considerable care, found that one of his patients lost ¾ ounce precisely at death;[96] another lost ½ ounce, with an additional loss of 1 ounce during the next few minutes, after which no further loss took place; another yielded very nearly the same result; and so on. Thus we have the old Egyptian idea of the weighing of the soul after death resuscitated in a very practical form in modern times—only with the medical practitioner in the place of Thoth, the great assessor of the Underworld! And it would be satisfactory to know how far modern observation of a normal soul weight corresponds with ancient speculation in the matter. It is curious anyhow to find that Fournier d'Albe's estimates are so nearly corroborated by Dr. M'Dougall; and we must await with interest further and perhaps more detailed observations along the same line.

Another line along which something seems to have been done by hard and fast science to corroborate the general theory of the extrusion of a cloud-like spirit form from the body at death, is in the matter of photography. Dr. Baraduc, in his book, *Mes Morts: leurs manifestations* (8), gives an account of photographs which he took of his wife's body within an hour after death and of his son's body (in the coffin) nine hours after death. When developed the plates all showed cloud-like emanations hovering over the corpses, not certainly having definite human outline, but apparently shot through by lines and streaks of light. And though here again the experiments are not conclusive, they so far are corroborative, and may be taken to indicate a direction for further inquiry.

This last I think we are especially entitled to say, on account of what has been already done in the way of photographing the cloud-figures (some of them very definite in outline) which are found to emanate on occasions from mediums in the state of trance. For notwithstanding the doubt which has commonly been cast on all such photographs and notwithstanding the very obvious ease with which cameras can be manipulated and shadow-figures of some kind fraudulently produced, the evidence for the genuineness of some such 'spirit' photographs is—to any one who really studies it—beyond question. The celebrated "Katie King," who appeared at seances in connection with the medium Florence Cook, and during a period of two years or more was seen by some hundreds of people—and especially studied by Sir William Crookes—was photographed several times under test conditions.[97] Professor Charles Richet, who when he first heard of Crookes' conclusions was convulsed with laughter over their supposed absurdity, afterward confessed his error,[98] for time after time he not only saw a phantasm ("Beni Boa") in connection with the Algerian medium Aisha, but obtained photographs of the same.[99] Dr. A. R. Wallace, in a long note, pp. , of his book, *Miracles and Modern Spiritualism*, gives a careful description of his own experiments in this line. Several different figures were at different times photographed in connection with Mme. D'Espérance; and the very detailed account, with illustrations, which she gives of these phenomena in ch. xxvii. of her book, *Shadowland*, must give the unbeliever pause. And so on. The evidence is so abundant, and so on the whole so well confirmed, that we are practically now compelled to admit (and this is the point in hand) that cloud-like forms of human outline emanating from a medium's or other person's living body may at times be caught by the photographic plate. And this is important because it removes the phenomenon from the region of the fanciful or imaginative and gives it automatic and objective registration.

That these forms occurring and occasionally photographed in connection with mediums are independent 'spirits' or souls is of course in no way assumed. They may be such, or (what seems more likely) they may be simply extensions of the spiritual or inner body of the medium. The point that interests us here is that their appearance in either case points to the actual existence of such an inner body, capable of becoming extruded from the gross body, and of becoming the seat and manifestation of intelligence. Further than that we need not go at present.

But it will be objected, if the inner or spiritual body is, as has just been supposed, of such a subtle and tenuous nature as to be in itself quite invisible, what connection can this have with phantoms that can be photographed, or that can be seen, or that can be actually touched and handled? This question—the question as to how an excessively rare and tenuous and invisible being may gradually condense and materialize so as to come first within the region of photographic activity, and then within the region of normal visibility, and so on into audible and tangible and material existence and operation, I shall discuss more at length in the next chapter. Suffice it here to point out that the general consensus of thoughtful opinion on this subject at the present time points to a probable condensation of some kind, and utilization of such suitable materials as may be to hand, by which the subtle inner body gradually clothes itself in an outer and denser garment. Whether with Fournier d'Albe we suppose a soul-like core to every single cell, or whether we take a more diffused and general view, in any case we seem compelled to believe that our actual bodies are carried on by organizing powers distributed in centres throughout the body. If by any means these vital centres were separated from the gross body, it would still seem natural for them to continue their organizing activity whenever they were surrounded with suitable material. And if, as seems likely, in the case of mediums and seances, a considerable quantity of loose floating organic material is commonly evolved from the bodies of those present, such effluences might be quickly caught up and condensed by any such vital centres present into more or less visible forms and figures.

If, by way of illustration, we were to suppose an army-corps to represent a gross body, then the officers, from corporals to general, would represent the inner or organizing soul; and all these officers together, though really being a 'body,' would constitute a mass so small and so scattered compared with the mass-body of the army, that in comparison they would be invisible, and might easily all pass out and away from the army without being observed. They might pass out and conceivably organize another army-corps elsewhere; but the result on that left behind (of which they were really the soul) would soon be seen in its complete disintegration and collapse. Now suppose further that in a neighboring nation, across the frontier, there was a great deal of disaffection existing—that large masses of the people there were out of touch with their own Government (the case of a medium in trance), and waiting for some one to come and organize them. Then it is easy to imagine the small group of officers aforesaid passing across the frontier (quite unseen and unobserved) and immediately on doing so finding ready to their hands a quantity of material just suitable for their activity. In a wonderfully short time the various officers would begin to organize the various departments of a new army-corps; the people would flock to their standard. Even in a day or two the faint outline of a new political form or movement would show itself; and in a week this might become substantial enough to exhibit serious manifestations of force!

The general application of this to the question in hand is obvious enough. But there is another point which it illustrates—a point which we have raised before. I am convinced that science will never yield any very fruitful understanding of the world, until it recognizes that *life* and *intelligence* (of course in the broadest signification) pervade all the phenomena of Nature. It is perfectly useless to try to explain human development, human destiny, mental activity, the forces of nature, and so forth, in terms of dead matter. No explanation of such a kind could possibly be satisfying. And more and more it is becoming clear that even what we call the inorganic world is as subtle and swift in its responses as what we call the organic. Many difficulties must inevitably arise in any attempted solution of the problem before us—that problem which is generally denoted by "the nature of the soul and its relation to the body"; but we shall never arrive at any harmonious view of the whole question until we are persuaded, and practically assume, that life and intelligence in some degree are characteristic of all that we call 'matter' as well as of all we call mind, and pervade the whole structure of the universe. We shall then see that the forces, for instance, which organize and direct the human body, even down to its minutest parts, are probably just as individual and intelligent in their action as those (to take the example just given) which organize and direct an army-corps.

CHAPTER XI

ON THE CREATION AND MATERIALIZATION OF FORMS

I HAVE suggested more than once, in preceding chapters of this book, and in *The Art of Creation* and elsewhere, that in the ordinary evolution of thought, in dreams, in trance and in other psychic states, we are witness of a process which is continually and eternally going on, by which the faintest invisible forms and outlines, the nearest cloud-currents of the inner soul, gradually condense themselves, pass into visibility, tangibility, and so forth, and (if the process is continued) ultimately take their place among the substantial things of the outer world.

Hitherto this thought has been applied in certain departments of inquiry, but I am of impression that its considerable and world-wide significance has been missed. Freud, in his *Traumdeutung*, insists that behind the dream, and inspiring its action and symbolism there always lurks an emotion, a desire, a wish. And Havelock Ellis (though with due caution) corroborates this. He speaks of "the controlling power of emotion on dream-ideas," and says, "the fundamental source of our dream-life may be said to be emotion." That is, an emotion (from whatever source) arises in the mind. Vague and cloudlike at first, it presently takes form, and (if in sleep) clothes itself with the imagery of a dream, which becomes at last vivid and dramatic and *real*, to a degree which astounds us. But dream-life is only a paraphrase, so to speak, of waking life—a phase largely corresponding to the waking life of children and animals; and in waking life the same thing happens. A wish or desire appears in the background of the mind; it moves forward and becomes a definite thought and a plan; then it moves forward again and becomes an action; the action creates a result; and the desire finally establishes itself or its image in the actual world. These emotions and desires and the images which sprung from them have a certain vitality and growth-power of their own. The figures in dreams move of themselves and concatenate with each other of their own accord—much as the figures do in a drama, as Coleridge long ago observed—and as the waking thoughts of all of us do, when we leave them a little to themselves and to go with loose rein. More than that; in some cases waking thoughts or passions become powerful enough to take possession of the whole man and embody themselves in his deeds—sometimes to heroic, sometimes to criminal ends. Or, taking possession of *portions* of the man, they precipitate conflict within him. The dramatic quality of dreams is evidently due to the different figures or incidents of the dream being inspired by different qualities or experiences of the dreamer; and in the waking man the same process may lead to tragic struggles and disintegrations of personality. In hysteric patients, where the central controlling power is weak, the very thought or fear of a disease may seize upon a certain centre in the body and stimulate there all the symptoms of that disease; or a mental image may seize upon a certain portion of the brain, and break up the personality with strange new manifestations.

In all these cases, and scores of others which we cannot consider now, the same action is taking place—by which invisible psychic and spiritual forces, for good or evil, are ever pressing forward into the manifest, and condensing themselves into visible and even tangible forms, or taking possession of existing forms for the purpose of expression and manifestation. And here we have (as I think will be seen one day) the whole rationale of Creation—we have the conception which brings into line the phenomena of the visible and material world and their genesis, with the genesis of thoughts in our own minds, and *their* passage into visibility and expression; we have the conception which unites the mental and material; and which makes the whole Creation luminous with meaning. Especially is this obvious to-day, when the theory of electrons is introducing us to a world as far finer and subtler than the atom, as the atom is finer and subtler than the tangible world of our experience; and is suggesting that these finest states of matter are of the nature of electrical charges, which, again, are quite analogous to mental states. Thus we have, almost forced upon us as the key to the creation of visible forms, the conception, of a process of condensation by which the most subtle thought and emotion does in course of time (brief or lengthy) tend to manifest itself in material shape, and may ultimately take on the most persistent and quasi-indestructible forms.

Reverting, then, to the subject of last chapter, we see that a 'spiritual' body—that is, a material body of a texture so fine and so swiftly plastic as to be the analogue of thought—is a conception quite in line with the conclusions of modern science; and that granted the existence of such a thing, it is quite in line also to conclude that it would tend toward condensation and manifestation in grosser and more visible form. I gave in that chapter some general outline of how such condensation might take place. I now propose to consider this process more in detail, and to give some evidence as to its actually taking place.

There is something perhaps a little comic about the idea of spirit photography—something which has thus helped to retard its acceptance. The busy photographer with his camera is so banal, and sometimes so obnoxious, a figure, that to think of him photographing a ghost, or the spirit of a dead relation, verges on bathos or the burlesque. Nevertheless, Nature does not attend to our canons in such matters, and in reality the thing is perfectly feasible and in order. It is well known that the photographic plate is most sensitive to the violet end of the spectrum—that it is this end which has the actinic quality. Moreover, it is known that the actinic quality extends *beyond* this end, and that there are ultra-violet rays which we cannot see, and which yet are photographically powerful. But the violet rays, as is also well known, are those whose light-waves are smallest—being only about half the size of the red waves;‖ and the ultra-violet rays are still smaller. Consequently, by means of the violet end of the spectrum, information can be got about small objects and infinitesimal details which would elude the more ordinary light. A particle, in fact, may be so small that it would reflect the violet waves, while it would be unable to reflect the red—just as a boat floating on the water will reflect and turn back tiny ripples, while it will simply be tossed about by good-sized waves. Advantage has been taken of this in microscopy, and by ingenious arrangements photographs of objects under the microscope can now be taken by ultra-violet light, so as to show the very minutest details.

The application of this to the question before us is clear. If there be a spiritual body, composed of particles so infinitesimal as to be—to begin with—far beyond the limits of visibility, yet gradually condensing and accreting to themselves other and subsidiary particles, there might come a time when such a cloud-form would approach the limit of visibility—the molecules of which it was composed having grown so far. It would be perfectly natural, then, for a body composed of such molecules to come into the region of possible photography in the camera through the ultra-violet rays *before* it came into the region of visibility to the human eye by means of ordinary light. And thus the seeming paradox may be accounted for—of the appearance of spirit-forms, or even thought-forms, on the photographic plate which are not yet discernible by the eye. At a later stage of materialization the form may of course yield an image both to the eye and to the camera.‖

Again, in this connection, it is often urged against the reality of spirit-forms, ghosts, and so forth, that they cannot bear a strong light; and this is held to dispose of all their claims for consideration. But what has just been said shows that on the contrary such an effect is just what might be expected. The delicate growing structure, whose particles were just large enough to reflect the smaller light-waves, might easily be broken up and quite disintegrated by the larger and more powerful weaves of a strong glare—just as, in fact, *our* forms, which can endure light, are broken up and disintegrated by the still larger waves of intense *heat.* Katie King, who, as before mentioned, appeared so many times in connection with the medium

Florence Cook, was frequently seen to fade away if the light was too strong. "At the earlier seances she could only come out of the cabinet for a few seconds at a time, once or twice during the seance; she had to go back quickly into the cabinet to gather fresh power from her medium, saying that the strong and unaccustomed brilliancy of the light made her 'melt quite away.'" And Nepenthes, that finely formed and beautiful figure which appeared in connection with Mme. D'Espérance, was more than once seen, by a large company assembled, to walk by the side of the medium up to the open French window at the end of the room and then to disappear as she came into the full daylight.

Photographs, it may be noticed, of forms appearing at seances, or in connection with sitters, vary from mere cloudlike masses without or almost without shape to very distinct human figures with much detail of feature and dress,—the same figure being often recognized in various stages of clearness and definition. And this is interesting because it entirely corroborates the observations made in hundreds of seances, and in other cases, in which a form is first distinguished by the eye as a faintly luminous cloud, and gradually grows in distinctness and definition till it becomes visible in all detail, and even tangible. Mme. D'Espérance, whose book, *Shadowland*, should be read on account of its intelligent handling and obvious sincerity, as well as on account of the remarkable phenomena reported, describes (p.) the first occasion on which a 'materialization' appeared to her:—"One evening, for some reason or other, we were sitting without a lighted lamp. The daylight had not faded when we commenced the sitting, but though it grew dark no one suggested making a light. Happening to glance over to the part of the room where the shadows were deepest it seemed to me that there was a curious cloudy luminosity standing out distinct and clear from the darkness. I watched it for a minute or two without saying anything, wondering where it came from and how it was caused. I thought it must be a reflection from the street lamps outside, though I had never seen it like that before. While I watched, the luminous cloud seemed to concentrate itself, become substantial, and form itself into a figure of a child, illuminated as it were by daylight that did not shine on it but, somehow, from within it—the darkness of the room seeming to act as a background, throwing up by contrast every curve of the form and every feature into strong relief." And in another passage she says:—"As soon as I have entered the mediumistic cabinet my first impression is of being covered with spider webs. Then I feel that the air is filled with substance, and a kind of white and vaporous mass, quasi-luminous, like the steam from a locomotive, is formed in front of the abdomen. After this mass has been tossed and agitated in every way for some minutes, sometimes even for half-an-hour, it suddenly stops, and then out of it is born a living being close by me."

Another figure—that of Yolande (a young woman)—is mentioned in the same book (p.) as appearing again and again out of such a filmy cloudy patch on the floor. Similarly, Professor Richet noticed over and over again the outgrowth of a figure (Beni Boa) from a white cloud. "Near the cabinet we could see, betwixt the curtain and the table, a whitish globe forming, luminous, and rotating on the floor; from this globe Beni Boa sprang." The figure would then walk round the room and disappear again; but after a time the white cloud would again form and Beni Boa reappear. And Professor Lombroso, alluding to this, says:—"This observation is of great importance, since it is not possible to attribute to fraud the formation of a luminous patch on the floor which transforms itself into a living being." Further, Lombroso says:—"Five photographs were obtained at these sittings by magnesium and chlorate of potash light, with a Kodak and with a Richard stereoscopic apparatus simultaneously, which fact excludes the possibility of photographic fraud; and all the plates were developed in Algeria by an optician who was unaware of what had preceded. On the plates appeared a tall figure wrapped in a white mantle" (and similar to the figure which the seven sitters present at the seances had seen).

I have alluded to this cloud-formation before as characteristic of an early stage of the appearance of these figures, and as suggesting a process of condensation going on. Lombroso, from various considerations which he brings forward (p.), seems convinced that the phenomena of these forms are largely connected with radio-activity. He says:—"It would seem that these bodies belong to that further state of matter, the radiant state, which now at last has established a firm footing in science—and which thus offers the only hypothesis which can reconcile the ancient and universal belief in the persistence of some form of life after death with the postulates of science which maintain that without organ there can be no function." This radio-active condition of matter is of course that finest and most active state represented by the electrons—in which each electron is excessively minute, yet moves at enormous speed, and carries with it an electric charge. It connects itself with condensation in this way, that "an electric charge assists vapor to condense," and "where ions (*i.e.* positively or negatively charged particles) are present in considerable numbers a thick mist will form whenever the space is saturated with vapor." And Fournier d'Albe says:—"In the physical theory of ionization and condensation we have become familiar with the fact that the smallest charged particles are the most effective promoters of condensation. In fact, it would suffice to extract a very small proportion of the innumerable electrons within the body to bring about a vigorous condensation in the moist air around it."

Thus it is quite probable that the cloud-formation, which in general precedes the manifestation of distinct figures, is due to condensation, and in part at any rate to a condensation of water-vapor on the accreting particles of the spirit-body. And this is made the more probable by the strong sensation of *cold* which so frequently accompanies these appearances, and which is a common accompaniment of condensation. Crookes, in his *Researches*, emphasizes this in connection with almost all the phenomena, and says they "are generally preceded by a peculiar cold air, sometimes amounting to a decided wind. I have had sheets of paper blown about by it, and a thermometer lowered several degrees. On some occasions ... the cold has been so intense that I could only compare it to that felt when the hand has been within a few inches of frozen mercury." Some such sensation seems to be quite a common experience, and the authoress of *Shadowland*, speaking of her earlier sittings (p.), says:—"It was not long before the same strange disturbances in the air began as on the previous occasion. I felt my hair blown and lifted by currents of air, and cool breezes played about my face and hands."

Thus (with the corroborating evidence of Crookes' thermometer) we may suppose that, after all, the cold airs and shivering sensations which seem so often to accompany apparitions may not be merely subjective to the observer, but may be real phenomena due to physical condensations taking place in his immediate proximity. Moreover, it has to be noted that the condensations may not be merely of water-vapor, but of other substances as well, namely (according to an opinion now gaining ground), of fine matter or effluences provided by the bodies of the sitters present (or some of them) as well as by the body of the medium. The passage last quoted from *Shadowland* continues: "then began a strange sensation, which I had sometimes felt at seances. Frequently I have heard it described by others as of cobwebs being passed over the face, but to me, who watched it curiously, it seemed that I could feel fine threads being drawn out of the pores of my skin." And in another passage the same writer describes the cloud which precedes a materialization as "a slightly luminous haze" which often appears "about the head, shoulders, elbows and sometimes the knees and feet (of the medium). Frequently it gathers slowly at the fingers, increasing in density till it resembles a slight transparent film of slightly luminous cotton wool." Further, she explains that it goes on condensing till it becomes cobwebby and perceptible to touch. The evidence generally seems to show that these clouds are of the nature of effluences from the medium or other person present; and the above quotation affords corroboration of that view and makes easily intelligible the great exhaustion from which mediums often suffer on these occasions. It suggests also that the condensation is by no means of water-vapor only, but of other substances drawn from the interior vitality of the persons concerned, and necessary for the building up of the apparitional form.

It is difficult in the case, for instance, of "Katie King," who, as already said, appeared hundreds of times during two or three years, or of Estella Martha, who appeared to her husband during five years and in or more seances in connection with the medium Kate Fox,|| not to believe that such figures are (as we should say) *really* the individuals they profess to be, and not mere thought-forms or images projected from the medium's under-mind. But whichever view we take, it is obvious that they are centres in some degree, of intelligent force or vitality, centres which, though in their essence rare and tenuous as thought or feeling, succeed in clothing themselves with a certain grade of corporeality by the use of the materials at hand, and in so coming into visible manifestation. And this general view is confirmed by the fact, so often observed, that when the same figure appears repeatedly, it does, as time goes on, acquire skill and adroitness in carrying out the process of condensation or whatever it is, which is concerned, and consequently comes into manifestation and activity more quickly and decisively. Also, it may be noted, and has often been observed (as in the case of the said Estella Martha and many others), that by practice the figure attains the power of enduring strong light—that is, its state of condensation reaches a point of solidity almost comparable with that of *our* tissues, which are not as a rule disintegrated by light.

The radio-activity of the 'inner being' also helps to explain the extraordinary manifestations of sheer physical force in these connections. Some of these manifestations have been so astonishing, that the fact alone has caused them to be disbelieved; but though, of course, fraud has played a part in such phenomena, and has to be guarded against, it is now quite evident that in a multitude of cases fraud does not enter at all.

Eusapia Paladino, for instance—though capable of little fraudulences—was obviously the seat of extraordinary powers not to be explained by these. Mr. Carrington, who made a special study of this medium, and who (as I have said before) has also made a special study of fraudulent methods in so-called spiritualism, vouches most strongly for the great exhibitions of inexplicable *force* in her vicinity—especially perhaps in the way of *levitations*. He says:—"Every one who has studied Eusapia's phenomena knows that practically every seance (for some reason) commences with table-levitations—this, whether they are wanted or not! It seems the necessary programme, and it is almost invariably carried out. Seeing them time after time, one can obtain a very fair idea of their nature and reality. And I may say that I now consider levitations as well established as any other physical facts. They are not open to the objection to which most psychical phenomena are subjected—that they cannot be repeated or induced and studied experimentally, as one would study other physical facts—for they can be induced and studied in just this laboratory manner. I have probably seen several hundreds of these levitations now, under every conceivable condition and in *excellent light*, and I consider them so far established that, as Count Solovovo said, "the burden of proof is now on the man who asserts that they are *not* real, not upon the man who asserts that they *are*." These are pretty strong words, and by a very responsible observer! And then Mr. Carrington proceeds with a detailed account of these and other physical phenomena.

Some years ago, the reports and accounts of such phenomena were generally at once dismissed as absurd and incredible; but by a remarkable coincidence the last few years have seen the wonderful development of the science of radio-activity—dating from the epoch-making experiments of Crookes, in 9 and earlier. These experiments, curiously enough, were worked out during much of the same period as Crookes' researches into spiritualistic phenomena, and have led to the shedding of much light upon the latter. For the new science developed from them, and already more or less popularized, compels us to suppose that the most enormous forces lurk all around, within the very structure of the atom itself—which of course is totally invisible to our eyes. The new facts observed, with regard to radium and other such substances, seem to compel the supposition that each atom is composed of an immense number (say ,) of highly charged electrical particles moving each with huge velocity—a velocity at any rate comparable to that of light. The dissociation of such atoms and the liberation of their constituent particles develops a fabulous energy. When it is calculated that one gramme or fifteen grains of matter (say the weight of thirty postage stamps) moving with the speed of light, would have energy enough to lift the British Navy to the top of Ben Nevis (Crookes); or that one milligramme (say the sixty-sixth part of a grain of wheat) at the same speed would represent the energy of fifteen million foot-tons (Lodge); or when, according to J. J. Thomson, the combined speed and mass of the electrons within such a milligramme of matter would total up to the work represented by a hundred million kilogram-metres; then we can at any rate see—whatever small variations there may be in the estimates—how immense are the potentialities of the tiniest points of matter; how each minutest atom comprehends, as Shelley says, "a world of loves and hatreds" (*i.e.* positive and negative electric charges); we realize that no manifestations of unexpected power are *per se* incredible; and we are indeed rather inclined to wonder how it is that these great inter-atomic energies do not more often force themselves on our attention!

It is evident that any such condition of being as we have supposed in the case of the 'inner' or 'spiritual' body, might afford means for the liberation—even from a single atom—of forces amply sufficient for the most 'miraculous' phenomena; and we are led to wonder and to ask whether it may not be the case that, after all, our gross bodies are really a hindrance rather than a help—whether it may not be true that the powers we could exert *without* them and independently of muscles and sinews and hands and feet would be far greater than those we actually do exert by means of these organs and appendages; whether, in fact, our gross bodies do not exercise a *limiting* effect, confining our activities to certain very clearly specified directions, and within certain very definite bounds? At any rate, this point of view is worth considering.

Certainly the well-established facts of telepathy, and the equally well-established facts of the projection of phantoms from persons dying, or passing through great danger, to friends even at a great distance, seem to show that the inner self of one person can send out rays or in some way impress itself on the inner self of another far-off person;|| and this, under the theory of electrons moving at prodigious speed, seems not impossible. For though there is a difficulty in supposing ordinary physical vibrations or radiations to reach effectively from one person to another (say a thousand miles away) on account of the law of space itself, which makes such radiations diminish in intensity as the square of the distance increases, yet in the case of electrical radiations it seems possible to suppose two people related to each other as positive and negative poles—in which case the radiations of electric charges would pass along lines connecting the two, and with comparatively little loss of intensity. Our present rather crude and lumbering bodies probably impede these subtle exertions of force; and the fact (already noted once or twice) of the greater activity of people in the telepathic or phantasmogenetic directions, when they are themselves outwardly in a dying or exhausted condition, seems to point to a considerable liberation of these powers after death.

On the other hand, the well-established facts of perceptivity at a great distance, or without the mediation of the gross body and the usual end-organs, point in the same direction. Considerable investigations have been made in this subject; and not only is the evidence for occasional clairvoyance at a distance well established, but there are curious cases in which the faculty of sight or of hearing seems to be transferred from its natural organ to some other part of the body, as of seeing with the knee, or the stomach, or the finger-tips. Myers gives considerable attention to this subject, and thinks that Professor Fontan's experiments|| "cannot lightly be set aside"; while Lombroso quotes an hysterical patient of his own, a girl of fourteen, who lost the sight of her eyes, but was able to read perfectly with the lobe of her left ear! Later on, in the same patient, the sense of smell concentrated itself in the heel of her foot! Mrs. Piper, as is well known, commonly raises her *hand* for the sitter to speak into, as if it were her ear. And in cases of somnambulism the sleepwalker will sometimes move securely through difficult or dangerous places with eyes absolutely closed. All these things seem to point to an aboriginal power of perception independent of the end-organs. It is obvious that if in the course of evolution our present faculties of sight, hearing, and so forth have been developed from the diffused sensitivity of an amœba or some such creature, then those faculties must have existed, in their undifferentiated state, in the amœba; or, to put the matter another way, the faculty of sight clearly does not reside in the cornea of the eye, or in the crystalline lens, or even in the retina itself; which are merely an apparatus evolved for dealing with the details of the matter. The retina catches the light-disturbance, and the optic nerve conveys it to the brain, and the brain-cells are agitated by it; but where does *sight* come in? At some point, doubtless, the agitations of the brain-cells or of their internal molecules are *seen* and interpreted; but the being that sees and interprets them may (we had almost said *must*) be capable of directly seeing and interpreting similar agitations in the outer world—that is, it may or must by its nature be capable of seeing the events of the outer world without the mediation of the end-organs or the brain. Frederick Myers, dealing with this subject, says:—"I start from the thesis that the perceptive power within us precedes and is independent of the specialized sense-organs, which it has developed for earthly use. 'It is the mind that sees and the mind that hears, the other things are blind and deaf.'"|| He thinks that in the development or unfolding of life on our planet "certain sensibilities got themselves defined and stereotyped upon the organism by the evolution of end-organs. Others failed to get thus externalized; but may, for aught we know, persist nevertheless in the central organs."|| It is evident—however we may explain the matter—that activities and sensibilities do persist and manifest themselves in the human organism quite independent of the ordinary and stereotyped end-organs, and this fact must go far to persuade us, not only that there is an inner, a more subtle, and a more durable body than that which we usually recognize, but that in some respects this latter body is a limitation and a hindrance to the activity of the former, and to the swiftness and range of the perceptions of the soul.

What, then, it will naturally be asked, is the object or purpose or use of our incarnation in this grosser body?—why, if there is such an ethereal or spiritual frame within, should it thus tend to accrete denser particles upon itself and ultimately to clothe itself in a vesture of so opaque and material a nature? It would be rash to attempt to answer so profound a question offhand—off one's own bat as it were; and still more rash perhaps to accept any of the ready-made answers which are offered in such profusion, and in so many different jargons and lingos, by the sects and schools, from the Gnostics and Theosophists to the most philistine of the chapels and churches. Yet if one may venture a suggestion, it would seem rather likely that the object and purpose and use of this process by which the soul is entangled in matter, and its operation and perception so strangely hampered and limited, is—limitation; that *limitation* itself and even *hindrance* are part and parcel of the great scheme of the soul's deliverance. But the further consideration of this I will defer to a later chapter.

CHAPTER XII

REINCARNATION

THERE is a good deal of talk indulged in, on the subject of Reincarnation—talk of a rather cheap character. One does not quite see what is the use of saying that the *ego* will be reincarnated again some day, unless one has some sort of idea what one means by the *ego*, and unless one has some understanding of the sense in which the word "reincarnation" is used. If it is meant that your local and external self, approximately as you and your friends know it to-day—including dress, facial outline, professional skill, accomplishments, habits of mind and body, interests and enthusiasms—is going to repeat itself again in five or five hundred years, or has already appeared in this form in the past; one can only say "impossible!" and "I trust not!" For all these things depend on date, locality, heredity, surrounding institutions, social habits, current morality, and so forth, which—though they have certainly played their part in the spirit's growth—must infallibly be different at any other period (short of the whole universe repeating itself). And anyhow to have them repeated again *da capo* at some future time would be terribly dull. But if you say "Of course I don't mean anything so silly as *that*," it becomes incumbent on you to say what you do mean.

Supposing, for instance, you had been planked down a baby in the Arabian desert, and grown up to maturity or middle age there, instead of where you are, would any of your present-day friends recognize you? Where would be your charming piano-playing, your excellent cricket, your rather sloppy water-color painting, your up-to-dateness in the theatrical world? Where your morality (with three wives of course) or your religion (something about "Christian dogs"), or where your British *sang froid* and impeccability? And if it is obvious that in such a case as this you would, owing to the changed conditions, be changed out of all recognition, much more—one might say—would this be the case if you had been born five hundred years ago, or were to be born again five hundred years hence. Your whole outlook on life, and its whole impress on you, would be different.

Of course I am not meaning, by these remarks, to say that reincarnation is in itself impossible or absurd; that would be prejudging the question. All I mean at present is that if we are going to study this subject, or theorize upon it, it is really necessary to define in some degree the terms which we use. I do not say that you, the reader, might not be reincarnated, but I think it is clear that if you were, we should have a good deal of trouble in following and finding you! It is clear that the *you*, so reappearing, would not be your well-known local and external self, but some deep nucleus, difficult perhaps for your best friend to recognize, and possibly even unknown or unrecognized by yourself at present. And similarly of some friend that you love for a thousand little tricks and ways. We all have such friends, and at times cherish a sentimental romance of their being restored to us in some future æon habited in their old guise and with their well-worn frocks and coats. But surely it is no good playing at hide-and-seek like that. The common difficulties about the conventional heaven—the difficulty about meeting your old friend who used to be so good at after-dinner stories, about meeting him with a harp in his hand and sitting on a damp cloud—is no whit the less a difficulty whatever future world may be the *rendezvous*. He would be changed (externally) and we should be changed, and it might well happen that if we did seem to recall any former intimacy we should both feel like strangers, and be as shy and tentative in our approaches to each other as school-children.

What do we mean by the letter "I"? and what do we mean by the word Reincarnation? These two questions wait for a reply.

The first is a terribly difficult question. It lies (though neglected by the philosophers themselves) at the root of all philosophy. Perhaps really all life and experience are nothing but an immense search for the answer. What do we mean by the Ego? It is a sort of fundamental question, which it might be supposed would precede all other questions, but which as a matter of fact seems to be postponed to all others, and is the last to be solved. All we can at the outset be sure of in the way of answer is the enormous extent and depth of the being we are setting out to define. We sometimes think of the *ego* as a mere point of consciousness, or we think of the ordinary self of daily life as a fragile and ephemeral entity bounded by a few bodily tissues and a few mental views and habits. But even the slight discussion of the subject in former chapters of this book (chapters vi., vii., and so forth) has revealed to us the vast underlying stores and faculties which must be included—the wonderful powers of memory, the subtle capacities of perception at a distance, or without the usual organs of sight and hearing, the power of creating images out of the depths of one's mind, and of impressing them telepathically upon others, the faculty of clairvoyance in past and future time, and so forth. The more we try to fathom this ego, with which we supposed ourselves so familiar, the more we are amazed at its labyrinthine profundity, and the more we are astonished to think that we should ever have ventured to limit it to such a petty formula and conventional symbol as we commonly do—not only in our judgment of friends, but even in our estimate of ourselves.

Reincarnation, as we have already said, can hardly be the reappearance, in a new life on earth (or even in some other sphere), of the very local and superficial traits which we know so well in ourselves and our friends—which are mainly a response to local and superficial conditions, and which mainly constitute what we call our personalities. If reincarnation does occur, it must obviously consist in the reappearance or remanifestation of some such very interior self as we have just spoken of—some deep individuality (as opposed to personality), some divine æonian soul, some offshoot perhaps of an age-long enduring Race-soul, or World-self—and in that sort of sense only shall I use the word in future.

In that sense the idea is feasible and illuminative. It explains the obvious limitations and localism of our personalities, as being more or less passing and temporary embodiments of our true selves; and it represents the latter as immense storehouses of experience from all manner of places and times, and similarly as centres of world-activity operating in different fields of time and space. At the same time, it presents various difficulties. For one thing, it poses the difficulty that for each of us this vast interior being is, as a rule, so deeply buried that both oneself and one's friends are only faintly conscious—if at all—of its true outline. And if one does not recognize this being, of what use is it to us? It is true that we sometimes meet people who at first sight give us a strong impression of far-back intimacy; but this is only a vague impression and hardly sufficient to afford proof of pre-existence. The only way of meeting this difficulty seems to be to suppose, as residing in this inner being or true self, another order of consciousness, faint intimations of which we even now have, and by which, as it grows and develops, we may some day clearly recognize our true selves and true nature.

Another difficulty is that (as already said) for any satisfactory sense of survival continuity of memory is needed; and we should have to suppose that the memory of each earth-life was continued into and stored up in this deeper soul or æonian self. Memory would not normally pass from one embodiment or incarnation to another, but each stream would flow into the central self and there be stored. And I think we may admit that this is by no means impossible. Indeed there are not a few facts (some already mentioned) with regard to the recovery of memory which make the mater probable. Though any given earth-life in a given form could not be repeated, the *memory* of such an earth-life, fresh and clear, may survive for an indefinite time in the crystal mirror of the deeper consciousness. And it is perhaps allowable to suppose that in this way, and with the lifting of the opaque veil of our present consciousness, we may some day come clearly into the presence of friends we have lost.

Here again, however, one has to be on one's guard. The mere fact of remembering (or thinking one remembers), in this our terrestrial life and with our terrestrial consciousness, some detail or other of a previous terrestrial life proves little—for, for aught we know, quite apart from our psychic selves, a streak of memory of more physical origin from some ancestor may have come down even several generations, and may be surviving in one's brain.‖ Indeed it is extremely probable that all organic matter carries memory with it, and not unlikely that inorganic matter does so too. If you thought, for instance, that you remembered seeing Charles the First beheaded—if you had a rather distinct picture in your mind of the scene at Whitehall, which you afterwards found by investigation to be corroborated in its details, you might at first jump to the conclusion that you had really lived at that time, and witnessed the scene. But after all it might merely be that an ancestor of yours had been there, and that the vividly impressed picture had somehow persevered in some subterranean channel of memory and emerged again in your mind. Even then you might contend that, since it was *your* memory, *you* must have been there—or at any rate some fraction of yourself in the ancestor, which now has become incorporated in your personality. There are a good many stories of this kind going about, which point to the possibility of the transmission of shreds of remembrance through hereditary channels, and suggest the idea of an active Race-memory, or Earth-memory, in itself continuous—a storehouse of experiences, but fed continually by the individuals of the race, and coruscating forth again in other individuals.‖ Indeed one can hardly withhold belief in the existence of such a larger life, or identity, 'reincarnated' if one likes to use the expression, in thousands or millions of individuals; but to be satisfactorily assured of the reincarnation of one distinct and individual person is another thing, and would almost demand that there should be forthcoming not only shreds and streaks of remembrance, but a pretty continuous and consistent memory of a whole former life.

Thus the whole question which we are discussing is baffled and rendered the more complex by the doubt as to what is meant by the word "I." It is clear, from what we have already said, that one person may use it to indicate (1) the quite local and superficial self; while another may have in mind (2) a much profounder being (the underlying self) whose depths and qualities we have by no means fathomed; while others, again, may be thinking (3) of the self of the Race or the Earth, or (4) the All-self of the universe.

I present these questions and doubts, not—as I have said—for the purpose of discrediting the possibility of Reincarnation, but by way of showing how complex and difficult the problem is, and how much *some* exact thought and definition is needed in dealing with it. At the same time, in pleading for exact thought I would also urge that in avoiding the whirlpools of sentimentalism we should be careful not to fall upon the rocks of a dry and barren formalism. Systems of hard and fast doctrines on these subjects—even though issued with all the authority of ancient tradition, and enunciated in a long-dead jargon—are the most unfruitful and uninspiring of things. They seem to contain no germ of vitality and are liable to paralyze the mind that feeds upon them. Besides the drawback—as I have pointed out before—that all such systems are inevitably false. Nature does not, in any department, work upon a cut-and-dried system; and while at the outset of an investigation we often seem to discern something of that kind, further study invariably discloses an astounding variety of order and method. It may be well therefore to be prepared to find a general principle of Reincarnation in operation in the world, but worked out, in actual fact, in a great variety of ways.

Certainly there comes into our minds, at a certain grade of their development, a deep persuasion of the truth, in *some* sense, of reincarnation—that "the Soul that rises with us, our life's Star, hath had elsewhere its setting." It blossoms, this persuasion, in a curious way, in the very depths of the mind; and in moments of inner illumination, or deep feeling, is discerned in a way that seems to leave no room for doubt. At the same time, it not only has this intuitive sanction, but it commends itself also to the intellect, because at a certain stage we perceive very clearly both how vast is the whole curve of progress which the soul has to cover from its first birth to its final liberation, and how tiny is the arc represented by a single lifetime—the two thoughts almost compelling us to believe in a succession of lives as the only explanation or solution. We are compelled towards a practical belief in Reincarnation, and yet (as above) we have to confess that our conception of what it really is, or what we mean by it, is only vague. This, however, is no more than what happens in a hundred other cases. The young bird starts building a nest for the first time, driven by some strange instinct to do so, and yet it can only have a very dim notion of the meaning and uses the nest will subserve when finished. And *we* found our lives on deep intuitions—of social solidarity, of personal responsibility, of free will, and so forth—and yet it is only later and by degrees that we learn what these things actually mean.

Referring, then, to the four alternative forms of the self given two or three pages back, and taking the last first, we may say definitely, I think, that as far as the self of each one of us is identified (4) with the All-self of the universe, its reincarnation is assured. Its reincarnation indeed is perpetual, inexhaustible, multitudinous beyond words, filling all space and time. Though the consciousness of this self is deeply buried, yet it is there, in each one of us. Occasionally—if even only for a moment—it rises to the surface, bringing a sense of splendor and of joy indescribable—the absolute freedom and password of all creation, the recognition of oneself everywhere and in all forms. But this phase of the self—I need hardly say—is for the most part hidden; and more common is it perhaps for the Race-self (3) to rise into our consciousness with more or less distinct assurance that we live again and are re-embodied in other members of the race to which we belong. The common life of the race carries us away and overmasters us with a strange sense of identity and community of being. Heroisms and devotions—as of men dying for their country, or bees for their hive—spring from this; and superb intoxications of joy. The whole of the life of primitive races and tribes, and the life of the animals and insects, illustrates it—in warfares, migrations, crusades, frantic enthusiasms, mad festivals—the genius of the race rushing on from point to point, inspiring its children, incarnating itself without end in successive individuals.

It is not so uncommon, I say, for us to be able to identify ourselves with this great Race-self, and to feel its thrill and pulse within our veins. And it might well be thought that, with these two forms of reincarnation (3) and (4) and the immense joy they bring, we should be content: even as all the tribes of the animals and the angels are content.

But it seems that man—when the civilization-period sets in, and after that—is not content. The little individual soul, now first coming to the consciousness of its own separateness, sets up a claim for an immortality and a reincarnation of its very own—apart from the Race-self, apart even from the Divine self. It demands that its *ego* should continue indefinitely into the farthest fields of Time—a separate entity, perpetually re-embodied. Can such a claim—in the light of what has been said above—be possibly conceded?

Certainly not. We have seen the absurdity of supposing that the local and superficial self (1) can ever recur again or be re-embodied in that form, except as a mere matter of memory (or possibly of a repetition of the whole universal order). And as to the underlying self (2), whatever exactly it may be, there are a thousand reasons for seeing that *as a wholly separate entity* the same must be true of that. I may refer the reader to *The Art of Creation*, the whole argument of which is to show that even the mere attempt to *think* of itself as a separate entity involves the human soul in hopeless confusion and disintegration; and I may remind the reader that we know nothing in the whole universe which is thus separate and apart, and that the conception, whether from a physical point of view or a psychological point of view, is impossible to maintain. That being so, there remains only to consider the possibility of the underlying self or individual soul being re-embodied—not as an absolutely separate entity, but as affiliated to some greater Life which shall afford the basis of successive incarnations. The problem is narrowed down, practically to the question whether the individual may not obtain some kind of individual reincarnation through the Race-self, or possibly through the All-self of the universe.

And here I will state what I personally think and believe about this problem, leaving the reasons for the present to commend themselves. I think that in the early stages—in animal and primitive human life—the Race-self is paramount; that each individual self proceeds from it, in much the same way as a bud proceeds from the stem of a growing plant, or even as a single cell forms part of the tissue of the stem; and is absorbed into it again at death. There are no individual and death-surviving souls produced, apart from the Race-soul. In the great race or family of bunny-rabbits, for instance—though there are certainly individual differences of character—just as there are differentiations of tissue-cells in the stem of a plant—it is difficult to believe that there are individual and immortal souls. Each little self springs from the race, and is an embodiment of it, representing in various degree its characteristics; and at death—in some way which we do not yet quite understand—returns thither, yielding its experiences to the stores of the race-experience. The same is probably true of the great mass of the higher animals, even up to the primitive and earliest Man. The Race-self in all these cases moves onward, upgathering the experiences of the individuals, wise with their united knowledge, and rich with their countless memories. And these tracts again, of experience, knowledge and memory, largely in a vague and generalized form, but sometimes in sharp, individualized and detailed form, are transmitted from the Race-self to its later individuals and offshots. Thus a kind of broken reincarnation occurs, by which streaks of memory and habit pass down time from one individual to another, and by which perhaps—in us later races—the persistent 'intimations of immortality' and persuasions of having lived before are accounted for.

I think that this process, of mixed and broken reincarnation, may go on for countless generations—the animal or animal-human souls so differentiated from the race-soul returning continually to the latter at death. But that a period may come when the Race-self (illustrated by the growing plant-stem) may exhibit distinct *buds*—the embryos, as it were, of independent souls—which will not return and be lost again in the race-soul, but will persevere for a long period and continually attain to more differentiation and internal coherence and sense of identity. In such cases any reincarnations that occur connected with these buds—though mingled with the race-life—will become much less broken than before, and more distinctly individual; till at last a phase is reached when such a soul-bud, almost detached from the race-life, may be reincarnated (or let us say 're-embodied') as a separate entity, with a kind of immortality of its own.

It must be at this stage that the characteristic human soul of the Civilization-period is evolved—which coheres quite firmly round itself, which protests and revolts against death, which even largely throws off its allegiance to the race-soul, and to the laws and solidarities of the race-life, and which has an enormous and overweening sense of identity and self-importance, claiming for itself, as I have just said, a kind of separate persistence. Here ensues, as may be imagined, a terrible period of confusion and trouble—the whole period of competitive civilization. The splendid claim of identity and immortality is made; but for the time being it is spoiled by what we call 'selfishness,' the mirror is cracked through ignorance. The Soul has disowned her allegiance to mere instinct and the race-self, and has yet not found a firm footing beyond—is only floundering in the bogs of self-consciousness and anxiety. What kind of Re-embodiment may belong to this period we shall best perhaps see when we have considered the further course of the argument.

For at last the process of transition completes itself. The human soul tossed about beyond endurance at length discovers within itself a divine Nucleus—a nucleus of growth and life and refuge and security, apart from its own fragility, quite apart from the race-life, independent of all the latter's laws and conventions and sanctions and traditions, independent of caste or color, of world-period or locality; and from that moment it (the soul) rests; it ceases (like the little rose of Jericho) from its desert wanderings; it radiates itself and begins to grow from a new centre; it is born again; it becomes the beginning of what may be called a Divine Soul. The man becomes conscious of an ethereal body forming within, unassailable or at least undestroyable by Death; and it is probable that, during this period, the subtle organism which we have already termed the Inner or Spiritual Body (ch. x.) *is* actually forming and defining and, so to speak, consolidating itself. The subtle body of a more perfect being is forming—a body which can pass unharmed through walls, fire, water, which can navigate the air and the planetary spaces, and which is built on the basis of the ether, itself the all-pervading life-substance of creation. A divine soul is coming to expression, an *ego* indeed, marvellously different and distinct from all other *egos*, and ever more majestic and unique growing; but rooted deep in the universal self, and ever from that root expanding and sharing the life of that self and of all its children.

With the formation of this divine soul, re-embodiment in its complete and adequate sense commences. The spiritual or subtle body formed within the gross body retains its characteristics after the death of the latter (many of which characteristics no doubt hardly gained expression in the one life just ended)—and passes on to other spheres, there to assume more or less definitely material bodies according to the sphere and the conditions in which it may need to move. It may seek re-embodiment on earth through ordinary heredity and childbirth—in which case presumably it enters into the growing germ, and moulds the development of the latter to an adequate, if not to a quite perfect and unsullied, expression of itself. If the reincarnation is to be into ordinary human and terrestrial life, this is probably the only available method. And it would seem that some advanced and well-nigh perfect souls do adopt this method, appearing as infants with a kind of divinity about them, and a germinal purity so great as to seem to proceed from an 'immaculate conception.'

But to most, in this stage, the toil and tedium of passing through embryonic life and physical birth and infancy may well appear intolerable; and since by now they have developed the subtle or spiritual body and the powers belonging to it, this ordeal is no longer necessary. The subtle body can—as we have gathered from former chapters—by a process of condensation clothe itself in a visible or even tangible vesture, and may function, at any rate for a time, in such outer or apparitional form without going through all the *abracadabra* of birth. If on the earth, such functioning can only be very temporary, owing to the difficulty here of the conditions, and of the supply of the necessary condensation-material; but in other and less ponderous spheres the difficulty is probably much less, and the formation of suitable bodies comparatively easy. Anyhow, it will be seen that reincarnation of this second kind is unitary and single in character instead of being divided or fragmentary; it is unalloyed instead of being broken and mixed; and a vision rises before us, in connection with it, of ever-growing forms and more perfect life-embodiments carrying out, one after another in long succession, the evolution and expression of each divine soul or separate ray of universal being.

Thus in answer to query two, on an early page of this chapter, we may say that there are two kinds of reincarnation proper—quite different from each other:—(1) That of the race-self in which the individual members of the race share only in a streaky fashion, each going back at death into the race-soul, and emptying its memories and experiences into that soul for general sporadic inheritance, but not for transmission in mass to any one later individual; and (2) that of the individual who has found his divine soul and evolved his inner body to a point where it cannot be broken up again; and who is thus reincarnated or re-embodied complete through successive materializations or condensations, in other spheres and without again undergoing the ordinary race-birth and death.

But though these two represent the normal forms of reincarnation, a third kind should be added which represents the transition from one to the other, and which is important for us because it mainly covers the period in which we now are—the great period of civilization. We saw how the soul of the animal is so close to the race-self, and so little differentiated from it, that it probably returns quite easily into the race-self at death; and this is likely to be the same with very early or primitive man. But when the distinctly human soul begins to form and to shape itself, it does not so easily forget its individuality and obliterate itself in that from which it sprang. And so we have the tentative, half-formed human soul, by no means well assured of itself, or certain of its own powers, and by no means perfect or contented, but much persuaded of its own importance and anxiously seeking reincarnation as a separate entity—and seeking this by the only means available to it, *i.e.* through heredity and birth as a member of the race.

It is a painful situation and experience. The soul, as human and not animal soul, is longing to separate itself from the race, to mark its distinction and independence—yet it has not, so far, found the divine nucleus which alone can give it real independence; and it can only gain expression and manifestation through the race-self and the ordinary paraphernalia of birth and death. It has learned no other way. Moreover, it is not yet completely differentiated from the race-self. It thus arrives at what can only be a very mingled and broken expression. Some father-stream and some mother-stream uniting, as it were, in the psychological neighborhood of this half-formed soul give it the desired opportunity; and blending itself with them it comes down into the world—a being of triple nature, embryonic and incompletely formed in itself, and utilizing as best it can the diverse elements of its maternal and paternal sources. Its career, consequently, and its life on earth are marked by a continual inner struggle and conflict—both physiological and psychological (due to the effort of the soul to bend the race-life and the elements of corporeal heredity to its own uses), and in strange contrast both with the hardihood and calm insouciance of the animals, in whom the race-life is untampered, and with the transparent health and serenity of those other beings in whom the divine soul has finally established its sovereignty.

Such, briefly described, are I believe the outlines of the reincarnation story. To put it in a few words, the whole process by which the race-self evolves and finally gives birth to myriads of free, independent and deathless individuals curiously resembles and may well be illustrated by a certain biological phenomenon common both in the vegetable and the animal worlds. Some growing stem or portion of tissue, perhaps of a plant, perhaps of a sponge or higher organism, is at first of a simple homogeneous character, fairly uniform and undifferentiated: but after a time it exhibits knobs and inequalities, which presently define themselves in a sort of *botryoidal* or clustered bud-like growth (as, for instance, in the spadix of an arum or the ovary of a mammal); finally these knobs or buds become entirely distinct and fully formed, and are thrown off 'free,' as seeds (in the case of plants and animals), or gemmules (in the case of sponges), or spores (in ferns and mosses), or as fresh and complete individuals in many aquatic creatures—in any case to enter on the beginnings of a free and independent life of their own. This kind of process, anyhow, is found in every department of biology, and it may well be that it extends upward even into the highest domains. The growing stem—proliferating cells without number, which are born and die in a kind of even uniformity within the limits of the stem—corresponds to the race-self in its early stages; the formation of knobs and buds in various degrees of clustered development corresponds to the partial growth of human souls out of the race-soul; and the liberation of the buds and germs corresponds to the liberation of the human souls into the freedom of a universal life.

CHAPTER XIII

THE DIVINE SOUL

THE liberation of buds and germs, as in the biological processes alluded to in the last chapter, is in general connected with sex, and brought about by its operation. And, similarly, I think we may say that the liberation of human souls and their disengagement from the race-matrix is brought about by love. I have already pointed out (ch. ix.) the intensely personal and individualizing character of human love. If one can imagine a love-relation going on between two members of a race—two portions, as it were, of the race-soul—at present only slightly individualized, one can see how the attraction to each other, the drawing away from their surroundings, the excitement, the agitation, all tend to further their growth as individuals—to give them form, apart from the matrix in which they are embedded, and definition and character. Of course all experience does this, but most of all and most deeply does love. It breeds souls out of the Race-self, and finally brings them away to an independent life. "It is for this that the body exercises its tremendous attraction—that mortal love torments and tears asunder the successive generations of mankind—That underneath and after all the true men and women may appear, by long experience emancipated."

As said in an early chapter, in love, though we do not know exactly what is happening, we are persuaded that something very profound and far-reaching is working itself out. And one such thing, I am sure, is the liberation of the soul of the lover—and, in less degree, the soul of the loved one. The tremendous experiences and convulsions, the profound stirrings, and the wrenchings from old ties and associations, do at last not only build the soul up into a distinct individuality, but they dig it up from its roots in the race and plant it out in the great Eden garden of emancipated humanity—the beginning of a new career.||

Another thing that I think is happening is that when love is strongly reciprocated the elements (as we have seen several times already), whether physical or psychical, pass over from one to the other and are interchanged—regenerating and immensely enlarging the life and capacity of each individual. This happens, I believe, in all grades of the universal life, from the Protozoa upwards. Two individuals drawn together interchange some elements of their being, and grow thereby into a larger and grander life; or may even in cases fuse completely into one individual person. As

Swedenborg says somewhere:—"Those who are truly married on earth are in heaven one Angel."

Thirdly, I think that the reciprocated love of two sometimes creates a *new soul.* We are familiar with the idea that the love (sexual) of two bodies commonly creates a new body; and there is an age-long tradition that the same is true in the world of souls. There is in that world also, not only regeneration but generation. "Love is the desire of generation in the beautiful, both *with relation to the soul and the body,*" says Plato; and Ellen Key, in a passage already quoted above (ch. iv., p. 61), says that "two beings *through* one another may become a new being, and a greater than either could be of itself alone." By love a new soul is sometimes generated which takes possession of both persons, and which suggests—as in the Swedenborg phrase above—that in some other sphere they really become one. And by love, we may also think, between man and wife, a new soul or soul-bud is sometimes created, which may descend into and vivify the physical germ of their future child.

To consider this last point a moment. The connection between heredity and the individual self is very mysterious. We acknowledge our descent, and what we owe, both mentally and bodily, to our parentage; but we are fain to think of our *ego* as something apart, something not to be confused with parents, and by no means merely derivative from them. Sometimes indeed there is great harmony between this *ego* and the parental inheritance, sometimes much the reverse; sometimes the line between the two is doubtful and uncertain. What is the explanation of all this? and what are the true facts of the relationship?

Does it not seem likely that, in the intense organic excitement which attends sexual union, this excitement—especially if strong love be also present—reaches right down into the soul-depths of each person, stirring these also, and the race oversoul at that point, most profoundly? So that, at the same moment that the germ of a bodily child is being fertilized, there is formed in the race-soul a soul-bud corresponding, which consequently descends into the physical germ and becomes its organizing life—the soul-bud thus being related to the souls of the parents, somewhat as the physical germ is related to their bodies? It springs, in fact, from a related portion of the race-oversoul.

Or again, does it not seem likely that in some cases, instead of a quite new bud being formed, the profound stirring of the race-life in that vicinity causes some older and more developed soul-bud—which has perhaps already had some earth-experiences—to wake into activity and take possession of the germ? In the first case mentioned the child born will be singularly like the parents, and in nature harmonious with them, with very little extraneous in its character, and with the fair prospect before it of a smooth and even career. But in this latter case, though the child will be harmonious with the parents it will have great depths beside, of authentic character of its own which will show out as time goes on.

And again, if deep love be absent, and consequently there is no special birth or awakening of souls in that region where they should be related to the body which is being born—what is likely to happen? Is it not likely that some other soul-bud, or soul which chance or other indication of destiny may bring that way, may enter in and possess the developing organism? And is it not likely, then, that strife and conflict and doubt may also enter in, causing a character of mixed elements, possibly leading to heroic developments, but also probably to a broken or tragic life-story?

As in the earliest and most primitive developments of life, so in the latest and most exalted, the soul is born through love, and through love it grows and expands. It may indeed be asked whether any other way is possible. Oppositions and conflicts may give form to the growing thing, and help to carve its outlines; but this gives it expansion. Every profound attachment necessarily modifies and enlarges the man. It pulls him out of his little orbit into a wider path—even if for the moment with some amount of eccentricity. Something is incorporated in his life which was not part of it before—something possibly which he did not before appreciate or understand. What we now are—whether mentally or physically—is an epitome of multitudinous loves in the past. The very cell-alliances which constitute our bodies are the records of endless heart-yearnings and romances (dating from far-back ages, and even now enduring) among a tiny people to us well-nigh invisible. And we may ask ourselves whether in the regions above and beyond our present life there may not be soul-alliances and even soul-fusions, by which we humans in our turn build up the very life of the gods? Plato in his *Symposium*, speaking of the strange desire of lovers for each other, makes Aristophanes say:—"But the soul of each manifestly thirsts for, from the other, something which there are no words to describe, and divines that which it seeks, and traces obscurely the footsteps of its obscure desire. If Vulcan should say to persons thus affected, 'My good people, what is it that you want with one another?' And if, while they were hesitating what to answer, he should proceed to ask—'Do you not desire the closest union and singleness to exist between you, so that you may never be divided night or day? If so, I will melt you together, and make you grow into one, so that both in life and death ye may be undivided. Consider, is this what you desire? Will it content you if you become that which I propose?'—We all know that no one would refuse such an offer, but would at once feel that this was what he had ever sought; and intimately to mix and melt and to be melted together with his beloved, so that one should be made out of two." And we may think—though this strange and intimate longing is never fulfilled, as we know, in the actual earth-life—that it still may possibly be an indication (as happens in other cases) of something which really is working itself out in the unseen world.

It was suggested, in the end of chapter xi. above, that limitation and hindrance are a part of the cosmic scheme of the creation of souls, and that there is a purpose in these things in regard to this mortal life. It was also suggested that the profound soul-stuff of which we are made is capable of infinitely swifter and more extended perceptions than those of which we are usually aware; and that there is a good deal of evidence to show that perceptive powers of this kind—quite independent of the usual end-organs of sight, hearing, taste, and so forth, still linger buried deep down within us. The question then naturally arises, If this limitation of faculty really exists as a fundamental fact of our mortal life, what purpose does it subserve?—And the answer to this is, I think, very clear.

It subserves the evolution of Self-consciousness and of the sense of Identity. It is obvious that diffused faculties and perceptions, however swift and powerful, could never have brought these gifts with them. It was only by pinning sensitiveness down to a point in space and time, by means of a body, and *limiting* its perceptions by means of bodily end-organs, that these new values could be added to creation—the local self and the sense of Identity. All the variety of human and animal nature, all the endless differences of points of view, all diversity and charm of form and character and temperament must be credited to this principle; and whatever vagaries and delusions the consequent growth of self-consciousness and selfness may have caused, it is incontestable that through the development of Identity mankind and all creation must ultimately rise to a height of glory and splendor otherwise unimaginable.

And not only limitation but also hindrance. These things give an intensity and passion to life, and a power and decisiveness to individuality, the absence of which would indeed be sad. As a water-conduit by limiting the spread of the stream and confining it in a close channel gives it velocity and force to drive the mill, so limitation and hindrance in human life give the individualized energy from which, for good or evil, all our world-activities spring. As the Lord says in Goethe's Prologue to *Faust*:—

"Of all the spirits of denial
The mischief-maker I most tolerate,
For man's activity doth all too soon unravel;
Of slumber he seems never satiate;
Therefore I gladly hand him to a mate
Who'll plague and prick, and play in fact the Devil."

Over a long period in this cosmic process this action, we may think, goes on. The vast and pervasive soul-stuff of the universe, in its hidden way omniscient and omnipresent, suffers an obscuration and a limitation, and is condensed into a bodily prison in a point of space and time; but with a consequent explosive energy incalculable. The Devil—*diabolos* the slanderer and the sunderer, the principle of division—reigns. To him, the 'milk and water' heaven of universal but vague benevolence is detestable. He builds up the actual, fascinating, tragic, indispensable world that we know. Selfishness and ignorance, the two great Powers of discord and separation, are his ministers; the earth is his theatre of convulsive hatreds and soul-racking passion; and our mortal life, instead of being the fair channel of cosmic activities, becomes a "stricture knot," as Whitman calls it, and a symbol of disease.

But this diabolonian process is only one segment of the whole. After the long descent and condensation and imprisonment of the spirit in its most limited and inert and self-regarding forms, after its saturation in matter, and its banishment in the world of death and suffering, the rising curve of liberation sets in, and the long process of its return. It is through love mainly, as we have seen, that this second process works itself out. From point to point through unison with others, by absorbing something from their experience, by sharing a wider life, the spirit's manifestation grows. By this the great tree of organic life spreads upon the earth; by this each race-stem multiplies its tissues and expands; by this the buds of human souls are formed; and by this the souls themselves are freed to independent life, and ultimately to circle again "dancing and sporting" as Plutarch says, "like joyous satellites round about their sun in heaven." There is continual Transformation; but there is also continuity from end to end. For every being there is continuance, but continuance only by change. Each soul is a gradual rising to consciousness of the All-soul; a gradual liberation and self-discovery of the divine germ within it. First the race-soul rising toward this consciousness, and then the individual souls thrown off, rising each independently toward the same. It is when the latter are moving over from their (instinctive and so to speak organic) community with the race-soul to a distinct and separate knowledge of and allegiance to the divine germ now declaring within themselves, that all this period of confusion and dismay, naturally enough, occurs—this that we have called the period of Civilization and the Fall of man—the period in which indeed we are now so fatefully involved. But it is in this period too that 'divine souls' are formed, and their feet first set upon the path of splendor.

Love indicates immortality. No sooner does the human being perceive this divine nucleus within himself than he knows his eternal destiny. Plunged in matter and the gross body he has learned the lesson of identity and separateness. All that the devil can teach him he has faithfully absorbed. Now he has to expand that identity, for ever unique, into ever vaster spheres of activity—to become finally a complete and finished aspect of the One.

CHAPTER XIV

THE RETURN JOURNEY

WE have seen that there is some reason for believing that, simultaneously with the birth or coming to consciousness of what we have called the divine soul, there occurs within us the formation of a 'spiritual' or very subtly material body. This body, if only composed of atoms, may easily be so fine and subtle as to pass practically unchanged through ordinary gross matter—the walls, for instance, and other obstacles that surround us. (At this moment there is an astronomical theory current that the stellar universe consists of two vast star-systems which are passing in nearly opposite directions right *through each other*.) If composed of electrons its subtlety and pervasive powers must be much greater. Moreover, its fineness and subtlety would make it difficult of destruction. The ordinary agents of death—physical violence, water, fire, and so forth—would, as already pointed out, hardly reach it; and it is easy to suppose that it might continue onwards and perdure in stability and activity for thousands of years. Even the Atom of matter, which is now regarded as a complex system of electrons, is supposed to have an immensely extended lifetime—nearly two thousand years in the case of Radium, and much longer in the case of all other substances; and if two thousand years or thereabouts is the minimum lifetime of an atom, it is not difficult to suppose that the lifetime of a subtle body composed as above described may be equally or much more extended.

During its lifetime, the radio-active atom, slowly disintegrating, pours out a prodigious amount of energy; and in the process apparently is transformed and takes on other characters and qualities. Radium for instance, or rather some products of its disintegration, are thought to take on the characters of Helium and of Lead. And similarly we have every reason to believe that the subtle body of Man is continually pouring out energy on all sides, radiating like a sun—pouring out mental states, sensible forms, influences of all kinds, even images of itself, and so continually entering into a wider life and touch with others, and undergoing a slow transformation of its outer form. At the same time—and leading to the same results—it is continually storing up in its recesses impressions and memories for the seed of future expression and development.

It may be imagined that the gross terrestrial body—though splendidly necessary for the localizing of the Self, and the establishment of the sense of identity, and for the electric accumulation of stores of emotion and passion, and so forth—acts on the whole in such a way as to greatly hamper and limit the activities of the inner body; and we can imagine that (as at death and under other special conditions) the liberation from the gross body is naturally accompanied by an enormous extension of faculty. The soul in its new and subtler form passes out into an immensely wider sphere of action and perception—so much so, indeed, as to make direct converse between the two worlds (the new world it is in, and the old one it has left) difficult to establish and very difficult permanently to maintain. The author of *Interwoven* says (p.) that the first body and the second body differ greatly in their chemical particles, "and so the same degree of sight and hearing is not possible.... *We* have just as much trouble to see the outsides of things as mortals have to see the insides."

Nor can we place a necessary limit to the birth of finer bodies. There may be a succession of such things. The electron brings us very near to a *mental* state; for whereas an Atom—conceived as similar to the speck of dust which one can roll between one's fingers, only much more minute—seems to have no relation to mentality, a tiny electric charge, capable of conveying a *shock*, comes very close! And at that stage the truth becomes apparent that the inner intelligent being in all things is the core, and the body is only the surface of contact—the surface, in fact, along which one intelligence administers shocks to another! With liberation from the gross body that surface may grow enormously extended, and it may become possible to *touch* or *see*, or to render oneself visible or tangible, to others far beyond all ordinary possibilities of contact or perception.

The succession of finer bodies may exist in any gradation, from what we call gross matter to the subtlest ether of emotion. At any rate we can see that at every stage there will be a finer body which is *more* of the nature of thought, and an outer and coarser which is less so. As the gifted author of *The Science of Peace*, Bhagavan Das, says:—"At each stage the Jiva-core (*i.e.* the core of the living individual) consists of matter of the inner plane, while its outer upâdhi (or sheath) consists of matter of the outer plane; and when a person says, I think, I act, it means that the matter of the inner core, which is the I, for the time being, is actually, positively, modified by, or is itself modifying in a certain manner, the outer real world." The inner film of matter (or mind), as he says, "is posing and masquerading, for the time being, as the truly immaterial self."

This central Self we can never *wholly* reach, but the movement of each divine soul is toward it; and the assurance and salvation of each soul is in the growing sense of union with it. The personal self can only 'survive' by ever fading and changing toward the universal. Our inner identity is fixed, but our outward identity we can only preserve by, as it were, forever losing it.

After life's fitful fever—after the insurgence and resurgence of passions; after the heart-breaking struggles which are forced upon some for the sake of a mere material footing upon the earth; after the deadly sufferings which others must undergo in order to gain scantiest allowance and expression of their inner and spiritual selves; after the mortal conflict and irreconcilableness of material and mental needs; the battles with opponents, the betrayal of friends, the fading and souring of pleasures, and the dissipation of ideals—the consent of mankind goes to affirm and confirm the conclusion that sleep is well, sleep is desirable. As after a hard day's labor, when the sinews are torn and the mind is racked, Nature's soft nurse commends a period of rest and healing—so it would seem fitting that a similar period should follow, for the human soul, on the toil and the dislocation of life.

It seems indeed probable—and a long tradition confirms the idea—that the human soul at death does at first pass, with its cloud-vesture of memories and qualities, into some intermediate region, *astral* rather than *celestial* (if we may use words which we do not understand), some Purgatory or Hades, rather than Paradise or Olympus; and for a long period does remain there quiescent, surveying its past, recovering from the shocks and outrages of mortal experience, knitting up and smoothing out the broken and tangled threads, trying hard to understand the pattern. It seems probable that there is a long period of such digestion and reconcilement and slow brooding over the new life which has to be formed. Indeed when one comes to think of it, it seems difficult—if there is to be continuance at all—to imagine anything else. When one thinks of the strange contradictions of our mortal life, the hopelessly antagonistic elements, the warring of passions, the shattering of ideals, the stupor of monotony: the soul like a bird shut in a cage, or with bright wings draggled in the mire; the horrible sense of sin which torments some people, the mad impulses which tyrannize over others; the alternations of one's own personality on different days, or at different depths and planes of consciousness; the supraliminal and the subliminal; the smug Upper-self with its petty satisfactions and its precise and precious logic, and the great Under-self now rising (in the hour of death) like some vast shadowy figure or genius, out of the abyss of being—when one thinks of all this one feels that if there is to be any sanity or sequence in the conclusion, it must mean a long period of brooding and reconciliation, and of readjustment, and even of sleep.

At first it may well be a troubled period, of nightmare-like confusion; but at last there must come a time when harmony is restored. The past lifetime is spread out like a map before one—all its events fall into their places, composed and clear. The genius, rising from the depths, throws a strange light upon them. "This was necessary. That could not have been otherwise. And that again which seemed so fatal, do you not now see its profound meaning?" The soul surveying gradually redeems the past. It comes to understand. *Tout comprendre, c'est tout pardonner.* It beholds, far down, the little fugitive among the shadows, pursued by the hideous and imbecile mask—the sense of Sin—and, recognizing a fleeting embodiment of itself, it smiles: for that mask has been seen through and is useless any longer. It beholds another—or is it the same?—pursued by the Terror of Death; and again it smiles: for *that* shadow—like the vast moonshadow in a total eclipse of the sun, which seemed so solid and all-devouring, has swept by; it has been passed through, and it was only a shadow.

And it may well be also that this whole process of reconciliation and adjustment and the building up of diverse elements into one harmonious being may occupy more than one such interval between two lifetimes; it may require several periods of incubation, so to speak. Looking at the matter from the physical side, and seeing how the inner and subtle body has probably to be formed during all this time—as in a chrysalis—and differentiated into an independent life, it seems likely that several intervals of outer rest and inner growth may be needed, and a series of successive moultings! But in the end, when the string of earth-lives is finished, and the reconciliation is complete, then the essential, the divine, self has become manifest, and is ready for a whole new world, a new order of experience, even to the farthest confines of the universe.

I have suggested in a former chapter that Memory—that very wonderful faculty—is probably our best test of Identity, our best test of Survival. If we apply this canon to the evolution of the independent soul out of the race-life, it may help us. When an animal dies, the group of memories, which is its life's-experience, probably passes back and is transmitted in a more or less diffused way into the general race-life or soul.‖ In the case of some higher animals it is possible that the memory-group thus returning may cohere for a time or to a certain degree, and not be immediately diffused. In the case of the higher types of *Man* it is probable that such group may cohere for a long time and rather persistently; and though embedded in the general race-life and memory, and much mingled with and modified by these, it may still form to some degree an independent centre of intelligence and organization (something like a nerve-plexus in the brain or body). It will form, in fact, what I have already called a soul-bud or budding soul, and will be capable of that mixed or partial reincarnation of which I have spoken—in which some truly individual streaks of memory will be mixed with general memories of race-life.

But after each successive reincarnation the group of memories returning—and allying themselves to the former groups—will necessarily give more and more definition to such budding soul, till at last the time will come when its individuality will be complete; its severance from the race-life will follow as a matter of course; and it will float out into the sea of the all-pervading and divine consciousness.

During this budding period of the human soul, which generally speaking may be said to coincide with the civilization-period of human history, the memory of each earth-life will go back into the race-soul there to swell the nucleus of the individual soul which is being brought to birth; but it will not generally revive into *evidence* in the next earth-life, for, being so deeply buried within, it will be too much overlaid by external layers and happenings to come distinctly into consciousness. It is not probably till the completion of the whole series of its earth-lives that the soul will resume all these memories and come into its complete heritage. Then, at some deep stage or state all its incarnations (clarified and comprehended) will become manifest to it—a glorious kingdom beyond the imagination of man at present to conceive. All its various lives it may live over again; but with as much difference in its understanding of their meaning as there is between an accomplished player's rendering of a piece of music, and a child's first stumbling performance of the same.

It will perceive that, in a sense, it has *pre-existed* from eternity. For though certainly there was a time when it first sprang as a bud from the Race, and entered into a gradually evolving and self-defining series of personal lives, yet that first bud was itself but a particular limitation and condensation of the Race-self; and *that* again, far back and beyond, a limitation through many intermediate stages of the All-self. It (the human-divine soul) will perceive that it pre-existed from eternity as the All-self; that it suffered in its time the necessary obscurations and limitations; that it abdicated the high prerogative of universal consciousness; and that it was born again as a tiny Cinderella-spark; destined to rise through all the circles of personal and individual life, and the enacting of the great drama of Love and Death—the great cycle of Evolution and Transfiguration—once more to the eternal Throne.

The glory of that Heaven where the All-self dwells radiant as the Sun, and each lesser or partial soul knows itself as a ray conveying the whole light, but in a direction of its own—we need not dwell on or attempt to portray. As the emancipated soul, just described, may include the personalities of many earth-lives and bodies, so there may be—probably are—larger inclusive selves, special gods, having troops of souls united to them in the bonds of love and devotion. Telepathic radiations, travelling as it were on lines of light, and with the velocity and directness of light, bring each unit into possible touch with every other, and over an enormous field. As the modern theory of electricity supposes that every electric charge, however small, or associated with the smallest atom, is connected by lines of force with some other and complementary charge *somewhere*—even perhaps at a practically infinite distance—negative with positive, and positive with negative; so the idea is suggested that in the free world of the spirit every need felt by one atom of personality anywhere is felt also and answered to by some complementary impulse and personality *somewhere*. In the bringing together of these needs and affections, in the recovery and the building up and the presentation in sensible form of all the worlds of memory, slumber infinite possibilities, and the outlines of endless situations and developments. The individual is clearly not lost in any 'Happy Mass'; but may contribute to the formation of such a thing in the sense that he comes into such wide and extended touch with others as to have a practically unlimited range of experience, memory, knowledge, creative power, and so forth, to draw on.

Nor is there any call to think of a *bodiless* heaven or bodiless state of being in any plane of existence. The body in any stage or state is, I repeat, a surface of contact. Wherever one intelligent being comes into touch with another—whether actively, by impressing itself on the other, or passively by being impressed—there immediately arises a body. There arises the sense of matter, which is in fact the *impression* made by one being upon another. The external senses, of sight, hearing and the rest, are modifications or limitations of more extended inner faculties, of vision, audition, and so forth. The actual world of Nature which we know, in the bodies of the woods and streams, and of animals and men, is built up out of the material of our senses; out of the kind of impressionability of which our senses are susceptible; but if these materials, of our sight and hearing and touch and taste, were altered but slightly in their range, the whole world would be different. They would create for us another world. And so, if these present end-organs of sense were destroyed, the soul, furnished with the inner faculties corresponding, would create another world of sense and of Nature, which would become the medium of expression and communication on that new plane, and the material of its bodily manifestation there. At present, owing to entanglement in the grosser senses, life is certainly in the main a matter of food and drink, of sex, of money-making, and the exercise of rather rude recreations and arts. With a finer range of sense, there would still remain the roots and realities of these things; the need of sustenance would still survive in the finer body, and the need of interchange and the indrawing of vitality; the hunger of union and of intercourse would remain—to be expressed in some shape or other; the delight in music and in beauty of form would be no less, though sounds and colors might be different from those we know; and all the faculties that we have—and others too that are now only embryonic with us—would demand their exercise and expression. Out of such demands and needs would arise a corresponding world.

I have suggested above (ch. xi.) how, deep in the subliminal self, there lies a marvellous faculty of producing visible and audible phenomena—Visions and Voices and Forms. Out of the depths of being these can be evoked, and bodied forth into the actual world.‖ In other words, each such Self, in its moods of power, can call forth its own thoughts and mental images with such force as to impress them irresistibly on others within its range—with such force, in fact, as to give them a material vesture and location. What we have said of the vastness and range of the human Under-self, of its swift interrelation with others, of the immensity of its memory extending far back into the deeps of time, must convince us that its powers of creation must be correspondingly wonderful. The phenomena exhibited by entranced mediums, and by hypnotized subjects, are only a sample of these powers; but they hint dimly to us that when we understand ourselves, and what we are, and when we understand others, and what they are, Time and Space and Estrangement will no longer avail against us; they will no longer hinder us from recognition of each other, nor hold us back from the spheres to which we truly belong, and the fulfilment of our real needs and desires.

Man is the Magician who whether in dreams or in trance or in actual life can, if he wills it, raise up and give reality to the forms of his desire and his love. It is not necessary for us feverishly to pursue our loved ones through all the fading and dissolving outlines of their future or their past embodiments. They are ours already, in the deepest sense—and one day we shall wake up to know we can call them at any moment to our side; we shall wake up to know that they are ever present and able to manifest themselves to us out of the unseen.

CHAPTER XV

THE MYSTERY OF PERSONALITY

IT will have been noticed that throughout this book there has been a tendency to return again and again to the question of what we mean by the Self. As I have said before (see ch. xii., *supra*), one might very naturally suppose that as the *ego* underruns all experience, and we cannot make any observation of the world at all except through its activity, the general problem of the nature of the ego would be the first to be attacked, and the very first to be solved; whereas, curiously enough, it seems to be the last! Only towards the conclusion of philosophical speculation does the importance of this problem force itself on men's minds. Nevertheless, I think we may say that in the department of philosophy it is the great main problem which lies before this age for solution; and that one of the greatest services a man can do is—by psychologic study and manifold experience, by poetical expression, especially in lyrical form, and by philosophic thought and investigation—to make clear to himself and the world what he means by the letter 'I,' what he means by his 'self.'

To the unthinking person nothing seems simpler, more obvious, than his own existence—and hardly needing definition. Yet the least thought shows how complex and elusive this 'self' is. It is one of those cases with which the world teems—a juggle of the open daylight—in which an object *appears* so perfectly simple, frank, innocent, and without concealment, and yet is really profoundly complex, deliberate, and unfathomable.

The most elementary considerations easily illustrate what I mean. When we speak of the ego, do we mean the self of to-day, or of yesterday, or of some years back—or possibly some years in the future when we shall have found the expression now unhappily denied us? Do we mean the self of boyhood, or even of babyhood? or do we mean that of maturity, or of old age? Do we mean the self indicated by the mind alone, or by the spirit, apart from the body? or do we mean that indicated specially by the body, or even (as some folk seem to consider) by the *clothes*? It would be very puzzling to be asked to place one's finger, so to speak, on any one of these manifestations as really and completely representative. Rather perhaps we should be inclined, if pressed, to say that our real self was something underrunning *all* these forms—that it required all the expressions, from infancy, through maturity, even to old age, and all the apparatus of body and mind, in order to convey its meaning; and that to pin it down to any particular moment of time, or to any particular phase of the material or spiritual, would be to do it a great injustice.

If so, we seem at once compelled to think of the Self as something greatly larger than any ordinary form of it that we know, as something perhaps on a different plane of being—underrunning, and therefore in a sense beyond, Time; and similarly underrunning, and therefore in a sense beyond, both body and mind. And this all the more, because, as I have said on an earlier page, we all feel that at best much of our real selves remains in life-long defect of expression; and that there are great deeps of the Under-self (as in chapter viii.) which, though organically related to our ordinary consciousness, are still for the most part hidden and unexplored. All, in fact, points to the existence within us of a very profound self, which so far we may justifiably conclude to be much greater than any one known manifestation of it; which requires for its expression the forms of a lifetime; and still stretches on and beyond; which perhaps belongs to another sphere of being—as the ship in the air and the sunlight belongs to another sphere than the hull buried deep in the water.

But we may go further in our exploration of the "abysmal deeps." We have once or twice in the foregoing chapters alluded to the possibility of the self dividing into two personalities, or even more. We have supposed, for instance, that at death the psychic organism may possibly split up—some more terrestrial portion remaining operant and active on the earth-plane, and some other portion removing to a subtler and more ethereal region. Are we—we may ask—and those others who propound the same ideas talking nonsense in doing so? Is it anyhow possible for a self to be active in two bodies or in two places at the same time? It may indeed seem impossible and absurd—until we envisage the actual facts; but when we do so, when we study the facts of the alternation of personalities, so much in evidence at the present time, when we find that two or more personalities, or coherent bodies of consciousness, may not only succeed each other in one human organism, but may *simultaneously* be active in the same, when we find that there is such a thing as 'bilocation,' and that the apparition of a person may come and deliver a message while the original person is far away and otherwise engaged, when we notice carefully our own internal psychology and find that we not unfrequently "talk to ourselves" and in other ways behave as two persons in one body—we see that the absurdity or unlikelihood of the suggestion may not by any means be so great as supposed, and that we may after all be forced to largely remodel our conception of what Personality is.

That one Personality should divide into two or more may seem to be foreign to our habitual views; yet we must remember that worms, annelids, and molluscs of various kinds commonly so divide; and though it is puzzling to think what becomes of the 'I' or 'self' of a sea-anemone when the latter is cut in twain and each part goes its way as a new creature, we must not therefore refuse to envisage the fact and the problem thus flowing from it. As to the Protozoa, which certainly exhibit signs of considerable intelligence, *fission* of one cell into two or more is one of the most normal and frequent events of their lives. The same, of course, is true of the elementary cells of the human body; the fission even of whole organs of the body is not uncommon, though more pathological in character; and the fission of the personality, as just mentioned, is quite frequent; and in some cases—as in the well-known case of Sally Beauchamp—very striking, on account of the furious apparent opposition developed between one portion and another.▯

The conception therefore of Personality must, it would seem, include the thought of possible bilocation—that is, of possible manifestation in two places at the same time; and it must not refuse the thought of inclusion—*i.e.* of one personality being possibly included within another—as of living and intelligent cells within the body.▯ Furthermore, we must not only allow *division* of self as one of the attributes of personality, but also, apparently, *fusion* with other selves. This may seem far-fetched and unreasonable at first, but on consideration we cannot but see that in one degree or another it is quite in the order of Nature. The Protozoa, of course, quite frequently combine with each other, and so make a new start in life; in the higher organisms the sperm-cell and germ-cell fuse completely for the conception of the offspring, and the organisms themselves fuse partially and interchange elements during the process of conjunction; and in the psychology of love among human beings we notice a similar fusion, and sometimes also almost a confusion, of personalities.

The little self-conscious mind (of the civilized man) no doubt protests against all this. It desires to think of itself as a separate and definite entity, distinct from (and perhaps superior to) all others; and it finds any theories of possible fission or fusion of personalities quite baffling and impracticable. Yet in the light of the All-self—the key-thought of this book—the whole thing is obvious, and there is really no difficulty, except perhaps in the linking up (through memory) of the continuity of each lesser self.

What we said in the last chapter, namely that "the personal self-consciousness can only survive by ever fading and changing toward the universal," must be borne in mind. Continual *expansion* is a normal condition of consciousness. Time is an integral element of it.▯ Consciousness must continually grow. Through memory it preserves the past, through the present it adds to its stores. The author of *The Science of Peace* illustrates the subject (p.) by asking us to consider the spheres of consciousness of various officials in a country whose departments more or less overlap each other: "There are administrative officers in charge of each department, whose consciousness may be said to include the consciousness of their subordinates in that department, to exclude those of their compeers, and to be in turn included in those of their superiors. The more complicated the machinery of the government, the better the illustration will be of inclusions and exclusions and partial or complete coincidences, and overlappings and communions of consciousness. At last we come to the head of the government, whose consciousness may be said to include the consciousnesses, whose knowledge and power include the knowledges and powers of all the public servants in the land, and whose consciousness is so expanded as to enable him to be in touch with them all and feel and act through them all constantly. An officer promoted through the grades of such an administration would clearly pass through expansions of consciousness.... Such expansion of consciousness, then, is not in its nature more mysterious and recondite than any other item in the world-process, but a thing of daily and hourly occurrence. In terms of metaphysic it is the coming of an individual Self into relation with a larger and larger not-self."

In the light of the All-self, I say, the difficulties disappear. It is the question of Memory (explicit or implicit) which seems to decide the limits of personalities and their survival. The One Self is experiencing in all forms, but the stores of experience and memory are kept separate. Here is a man who has a Town house and a Country house and an Italian villa. When he changes his abode from one to the other he becomes to a great extent a different person. His surroundings and associations, his pursuits and occupations, his dress and habits, his language may be, are changed. It may even happen that each of his three lives goes on growing and expanding after its own pattern, and becoming more and more different from the two others; and yet the ultimate person behind them all remains the same. Is it not possible that the lives of us human beings may go on expanding and growing each according to its own law, and yet the ultimate individual or Being behind them all may remain the same?

If a worm be supposed to have memory (and worms no doubt have memory in some degree), then it might well be supposed that, if divided in two, each of the parts would inherit the said memory complete. But from that moment the experiences of the two portions, moving in different directions, would bifurcate, and the future stores of memory would be different. Thus we should have a bifurcation of the stream of memory, and a bifurcation of personality—until ultimately, as time went on, and the common memory faded into the background, the two new personalities would begin to feel themselves almost quite separate. Is not this again something like what may have happened to ourselves from Creation's birth? The stream of life has bifurcated and bifurcated till we have lost our common memory and have become convinced of the absolute separation of our personalities one from the other.

On the other hand, the conjunction and fusion of two streams of memory in one is as probable and intelligible as the bifurcation of one into two. Two protozoa fuse; but the race-self in one is the same as in the other, and in reality the process is only a fusion of organic memories and experiences. A man who had been in the habit of changing every year from his Town to his Country house might some day find it convenient to combine his establishments in one suburban residence. Certainly if he had so far forgot *himself* that in changing houses he had always *quite* changed his memories, then it would seem impossible to him to combine the two lives in one. Otherwise there would be no difficulty in the process. The stores of one establishment, with their associations and memories would after a time (and not without some maturation-divisions and extrusions!) be got into relation with the stores of the other establishment; and the two bodies of memory and association would settle down together.

All this seems to suggest to us that our conception of personality must be considerably altered from its ordinary form, and rendered more fluent, in order to tally with the real facts. There is no such thing as a fixed and limited personality, of definite content and character, which we can credit to our account, or to the account of our friends. All is in flux and change, the consciousness ever enlarging, the *ego* which is at the root of that consciousness ever growing in the knowledge of itself as a vital portion of the All-self. That last alone is fixed; that alone as the 'universal witness' is permanent. But the streams of memory and experience, by which from all sides that central fact and consciousness is reached, are infinite in number and variety. It is in the continuity of a stream of memory that what we call personality must be supposed to consist; and when this continuity covers not only a single life, but extends from life to life, then we must find a new name for the persistent being and call him not a personality, but, if we will, an *individuality*. Such individualities must exist by millions and billions; they must be as numerous as all the possible lines of experience (and these are quasi-infinite in number) by which the soul may grow from its birth in the simplest speck of matter to its realization of divine and universal life. The author (Bhagavan Das) of *The Science of Peace* illustrates this infinitude of individualities, and how they are all contained in the All-self, and each in a sense as an aspect of the One, by the simile of a museum or gallery. "If a spectator," he says (p.), "wondered unrestingly through the halls of a vast museum or great art gallery, at the dead of night, with a single small lamp in one hand, each of the natural objects, the pictured scenes, the statues, the portraits, would be illumined by that lamp in succession for a single moment, while all the rest were in darkness, and after that single moment would fall into darkness again. Let there now be not one but countless such spectators, as many in endless numbers as the objects of sight within the place, each spectator wandering in and out incessantly through the great crowd of all the others, each lamp bringing momentarily into light one object, and for only that spectator who holds that lamp." Then he goes on to say that each line or succession of experiences might represent an individuality; each individuality in the end would reach the totality of experience, but in a different order and in a different manner from any other; and all the individualities would all the time—though changing themselves—remain within the unchanging intelligence of the absolute, and would only be exploring that intelligence each in a different order. "For," he again says (p.), "an individuality can no otherwise be described, discriminated and fixed, than by enumerating the experiences of that individual, by narrating its biography."

We may also illustrate the matter by the conception of a Tree. A single leaf at the end of a twig may seem to have a little separate self of its own; but it is very ephemeral. It perishes with the season and another leaf takes its place. There is a deeper self, in the twig, which endures, and from which new leaves spring. And again the twig springs from a small spray, which is the source of other twigs and leaves. Should the leaf desire to trace its complete and total self it would have to follow its life-line through the twig and the spray, to the branch, and so right down to the central trunk. It could not stop at any halfway point, and say, This is my final self. But on its way to the trunk, at different points, it would find that its sap or life was flowing into other twigs and leaves, as well as the twig and leaf first mentioned. It would come into relation, so to speak, with other bodies beside the first. If we were to call the first leaf and twig a personality we should have to call some deeper self involving many twigs and leaves an Individuality, and so on to the All-self of the tree. The self of every leaf would approach the main trunk along a different line, and through various ranges of individuality; but all would ultimately participate in one whole.

I think some such view is clearly the most satisfactory way of looking at the matter. We are all essentially one; our differentiation from each other does not consist in differences in the central ego, but in the different lines of experience and memory. We can none of us boast, at any point, of a rounded, definite and stationary self, apart from all others; but we are all approaching the universal from different sides. Yet, also, it is perfectly true that consciousness is born in us first *through* our very limitations. Through the very obstacles that surround us, and through the things that seem to divide us from others, first simple consciousness and then self-consciousness are born. Then comes a time when the limitations and the barriers become intolerable. The soul that at first gloried in them comes to find the burden of self-consciousness too great. Why should it be forever John Smith? As Mrs. Stetson says:—

"What an exceeding rest 'twill be
When I can leave off being Me!...
Done with the varying distress
Of retroactive consciousness!...
Why should I long to have John Smith
Eternally to struggle with?"

When the consciousness arises of this fact, that we need not be tied to John Smith forever—that our real self is far vaster, and essentially one with others, then in each of us the Divine Soul is born; a vista of glory and splendor opens in front, and on all sides the barriers fall to the ground. On the way to this supreme conclusion the stream of memories which one calls oneself may of course take on form after form; it may bifurcate, or it may fuse with other streams. That does not very much matter. The real identity, once established, can hardly be lost. For every leaf there is a channel of sap which connects it with the main trunk. Personality is real, but it yields itself up in the greater Individual of which it is the expression; and the individual or divine soul is real—enduring perhaps many thousands of years—but it yields itself up ultimately in the All. Finally, in that union, Memory itself, in its mortal form, ceases, for it is swallowed up in actual realization, in the power of actual presence in all space and time. The divine soul which has thus completed its union needs memory no more. It is there wherever it desires to be. As the author of *Siderische Geburt* (Berlin, 0) says, "We mortals are separated from the divine all-embracing universal Vision; and Memory is only a first glimmering reawakening—a beginning of renewed seraphic life and a coming into relation with all that lies beyond the little world-corner of our presence."||

At first sight, and to one who does not yet realize the inner unity of being, these views on the nature of Personality and Individuality may appear strange and even painful. For such a person the thought of the dissociation of his 'self,' of its separation into two or more parts—either in life or in death—and the divergence of the two parts from each other, must be grotesque and terrible, and verging even towards madness. And so also must be the thought of the possible dissociation of the personalities of his friends. And yet it may be necessary for us at length and by degrees to understand and assimilate such a view. Certain it is that, as we come to understand it, we shall see that any dissociation that may occur can only be of the superficial elements—something of the nature of a divergence of the chains of memory; and that dissociation of the real and intimate self is a thing quite impossible. We shall see that by degrees the self may learn to deal with such dissociations, and to express itself in various guises, and in more than one personality at a time. If, for instance, there does occur at death a certain break-up of the psychic organism—if the animal soul, and the human soul, and the divine soul do to a certain extent part from each other and go along different ways, we may see that it is quite possible that the personal stream of memory may correspondingly branch in different directions. One portion of the consciousness, having always been animal and terrestrial in character, may identify itself mainly with the animal vitality of the residue and its corresponding memories—and may persevere for some time as a wandering passional centre, liable to attach itself to the organisms of living folk, or to figure as a 'ghost' of very limited activities and occupied with eternal repetitions of the same action; another portion, more distinctly human, may linger in some intermediate state, partly in touch with the earth-life and the souls of mortal friends, yet partly drawn onward into wider spheres; and may function on for a long time in a kind of dreamland—creating perhaps the objects of its own consumption till it wearies of them, or building up imaginative worlds of occupations and activities similar to our own, as in "the happy hunting grounds" of Indians, or the worlds described from time to time by mediumistic 'controls.' And again a third portion may pass into that far wider and grander state of being which we have described—that of the 'divine' soul which recognizes its equality and unity with all others, and its freedom of the whole universe. In all these cases the main stream of memory, branching, must pour itself into the section of life which follows, and render the latter quite continuous with the former—though naturally with some differences, both in the memories transmitted, and in the degrees of community, in each case.

We may apply these considerations to the question of the messages and apparitions from the unseen world which have been alluded to in former chapters. How far or in what special way these communications really represent the active and continuing consciousness of our departed friends is a question which is generally admitted to be most doubtful and difficult. And its difficulty is not lessened, I think, by our conclusions (so far) on the nature of Personality. If the stream of a man's earth-life memory may diverge at death into two or more streams, then it must remain difficult for us to say whether the communication which is coming to us proceeds from a mere overflow of that stream, which has eddied itself, so to speak, into the brain of the medium; or from some 'astral' shell of the departed one, which has already begun decaying and dissipating, in our atmosphere; or again from the true soul of the man which is pushing forward into the world beyond. Probably we do not yet know enough about the matter to form decisive judgments. In either case the memory exhibited may be surprisingly perfect. And it seems to me that in most cases nothing but personal evidence and personal detail, even down to the minutest points, can decide—and even then not in such a way as to decide for others. And perhaps it is best and most natural so. In our world of ordinary life it is so. If an apparent stranger turns up from the other side of the earth and claims a far-back acquaintance; if another makes the same claim over the telephone; if a known friend behaves strangely, and we are in doubt whether to attribute his conduct to *bona fides* or to incipient madness; in these and a thousand other cases, personal relationship and personal understanding (though by no means unerring) count for more than all science and legal proof. And perhaps this is the healthiest way to take the subject: not to be over-curious or speculative or sentimental, but where solid help and a permanent and useful relationship seems to be gained, there to accept the communications as so far commending and justifying themselves.

If, as I have just said, there is something a little disquieting and even terrible in the thought that our personality may thus be subject to rupture or dissociation into two or more portions, that matter after all depends upon how we look upon it—whether from below, as it were, or from above. There is nothing particularly terrible in the thought that our bodily organs and parts—our "Little Marys," and so forth—may have (probably do have) very distinct personalities of their own. We look down upon them, so to speak, and include them. And we shall one day no doubt, and in the realization of our greater selves, have the splendid experience of including two (or more) bodies—of having them at our service, and available for command and expression. Even now we are sometimes conscious of having one envelope of a more ethereal and intense nature, swift and far-reaching both in movement and perception in the innermost regions, and another more local body, in touch with terrestrial life. And there would be nothing surprising or dreadful in finding, after death, that an ethereal and a terrestrial body were both still at our command—though both perhaps more developed and more differentiated from each other than at present;—or even that we might be capable of inhabiting several such bodies.

It is of course puzzling, under our ordinary conceptions of Space and Time, to imagine how it could be possible to deal with several bodies at the same time; but in reality it is no more puzzling than the problem which we habitually solve every day and every hour of our lives. How do we, for instance, deal with and dispose the activities of our hands and our feet and our eyes and our brain, with simultaneous care, say, in walking through the streets? We inhabit these separate organs, these distinct personalities, simultaneously, and ordain their movements and gather in their perceptions by the act of *attention.* Attention in the world of the spirit corresponds to *extension* in the physical world. Whatever your spirit attends to, that some physical radiation from yourself extends to. And similarly if you had bodies in different worlds and regions, by the simple act of attention your spirit would reach them. Nevertheless—to return to the one body and the various organs, like hands and feet and eyes, which we seem to have under control—it is clear that our minds could not possibly overlook all the details of their management, unless there were some general ordaining spirit in the body which was in close touch and sympathy, and ready to act with and aid us; and similarly it is clear that we could not ordain and organize any movement of a secondary body at a distance—even though 'belonging' to us—unless there were a spirit, in that body and the intervening spaces, in touch and sympathy with ours. It is the knowledge that there is such a community of life, such an abounding Self, which gives the 'divine' soul its great joy and its great power—"for whatever he desires, that he obtains from the Self." He who knows has indeed the freedom of the universe, and of all its powers—who knows that the Spirit of the whole *is* his own.

It is natural therefore to suppose that that portion of the consciousness which has circled and centred very definitely and conclusively round the All-self—or such aspect of the same as specially belongs to it; or (what perhaps comes to the same thing) has circled very definitely round the divine soul of a loved one; will pass through death easily and without much loss of continuity. It will with its attendant memories pass easily and continuously into the inmost sphere; or (to put the matter in another way) *remaining* in that sphere it will simply become aware that a mass of husks have been shed off, which clouded it. It will become aware of the glorious state of being to which it has always implicitly belonged, and of its connection with not one only but many bodies.

It may be—and I think one almost feels that it must be—that the most intimate self of any of us cannot be realized short of externalization in a vast number of separate manifestations or lives. One has the impression with regard to one's body, that "this is one of my bodies"; or that "this body represents a portion of myself"; but one does *not* feel "this body represents my total, complete and final self." And as we have just suggested that in a more intimate state of being we may become distinctly aware of having relation to several bodies simultaneously, so the world-old doctrine of reincarnation in its general form has long suggested that our most intimate selves are related to a great number of bodies in *succession* to each other in Time. The higher or inner Individual—of agelong and æonian life—is reincarnated (it is said) thousands of times; thus to embody that aspect of the Divine which it represents.

These embodiments may be in forms by no means resembling each other—though doubtless there will be a thread of similarity running through; and one embodiment may have little idea (except in moments of inspiration) of its relation to the others, or of any continuity of memory between itself and the others. Yet the memories of these lives and embodiments passing into the inner sphere are ultimately gathered together and drawn up to constitute that most glorious world of each Being of which we have spoken—a world in which each overlooks and ordains its various lives and manifestations as from a mountain-top. These are indeed "the ageless immortal gods who seek ever to come in the forms of men"—whom we ever and anon seem to feel and hear knocking at the inner door of our little local selves, as though they would gain admittance and acknowledgment.

CHAPTER XVI

CONCLUSION

AND so we seem to find—in the farthest and loftiest reaches of life, as in its first beginnings—Love and Death strangely linked and strangely related. Changing their form but not their essence they accompany us to the last; and we forebode them, in the final account, as no longer the tyrannous and often terrible over-lords of our mortal days, but rather our most indispensable companions without whom life in its higher ranges could not well be maintained.

For a time, certainly, we cling to our limited and tiny self-life and consciousness; and deem that all good resides in the careful guarding of the same. But again there comes a time when the bounds of personality confine and chafe beyond endurance, when an immense rage sweeps us far out into the great ocean; when to save our lives we deliberately lose them; when Death becomes a passion even as Love is.

The mystery of mortal life clears, or dissolves away, by our passing in a sense beyond personality; and the hour arrives when we look down on these local days, these self-limitations, as phases—phases of some far vaster state of being. Death is the necessary door by which we pass from one such phase to another; and Love is even a similar door.

Growing silently within there emerges at last something which has its home in the great spaces, which dives under and through Death, and is the companion of Titanic and Cosmic beings; something strangely surpassing all barriers and limits, and strangely finding identity by fusing and losing it in the life of others; something which at times seems almost mockingly to abandon its own identity and rise creative in new forms—sporting in the great ocean; and yet can somehow instantly recall its past and the tiny limits from which it first sprang—trailing forever with it the wonderful cloud-wreaths of earth-memory and association, and the myriad fragrance of personal remembrance. "What are thou then?" says the poet, addressing his departed friend:—

> "What art thou then?—I cannot guess;
>
> But tho' I seem in star and flower
>
> To feel thee some diffusive power
>
> I do not therefore love thee less."

Even in the farthest spheres the poignant syllables 'I' and 'Thou' will surely still be heard; and a thousand deaths shall not avail to exhaust their meaning or to make of Love a pale and cold abstraction.

The memory of the earth-life and of personal identity is never lost; but it passes out into that far greater form, the memory and resumption into a coherent Whole of many lives, and the sense of an Individuality which has value because it is merged in and is an expression of the All. Memory indeed changes from being the faint dream-shadow that we know, of things in the past, to being the things *themselves*, actual and ever present at our command; and with this finding of the inner soul and heart's core of all beings it becomes possible to live over again with them the days gone by, in all detail and with ever deeper understanding of their true meaning.

The supra-liminal returns into harmony with the subliminal; the individual life and the mass-life are reunited. With the overpassing of the local and terrestrial self we are liberated into a fluid region where a thousand personalities yield their secrets and their co-operation into our hands. With the releasing of our attention from personal objects and terrestrial gains, materials and people correspondingly cease to obstruct. They find nothing which they *can* obstruct! The body moves freely about the world; life ceases to be the 'obstacle race' and the queer perpetual vista of barricades which it mostly now is; and *a fortiori* the soul moves freely, because truly for the redeemed soul it is possible to feel that all things and creatures are friendly, all beings a part of itself. These and many other such realizations are indeed possible now—even in our present terrestrial state—under those rare conditions when the divine creature which is within the mortal body achieves a momentary deliverance, and under which we sometimes pass out of our little mundane dream into that other land where the great Voices sound and Visions dwell.

APPENDIX

SUMMARY OF CHAPTER II

1. Every kind of cell or other organism has a natural limit of size (dependent partly on the relation between surface and volume).

2. When that limit is reached, superfluity of nutrition and growth tends to bring about Reproduction.

3. Reproduction begins with simple division or budding.

4. Conjugation in its primitive form (as among protozoa where there is no distinction of sex) takes place between similars, and is an exchange to some degree of cell-contents.

5. It apparently affords a superior nutrition, and is a kind of Regeneration, essential to the continued health of the species, and favorable to reproduction.

6. Hunger and Love are thus related at this stage.

7. Later, conjugation takes place between dissimilars (of the same species); and the distinct phenomena of sex appear—of male and female.

8. Reproduction by simple division or budding leads to a kind of 'immortality,' since each descendant cell is continuous, in a sense, with the original one.

9. This simple division or virgin-birth process may go on to many generations—even to hundreds among the Protozoa.

10. But since at some time or other conjugation is apparently necessary in order to restore vitality, the immortality at this point ceases to be an individual immortality, and becomes rather a joint or racial immortality.

11. The main thing in conjugation would appear to be that the two factors should be complementary to each other, however differentiated, so that in their union the whole race-life should be restored, and the Regeneration therefore be complete.

12. The special sex-differentiation called male and female depends on the separation of the active from the sessile qualities (and other qualities respectively related to each) into two great branches.

13. Since the female takes the sessile part she appears sometimes as the goal and object of conjugation, and the more important factor; but actual

observation so far shows each factor, male and female, to be equally important.

14. In the fertilized ovum there are an equal number of chromosomes derived from each parent; and if the female provides the shrine in which the new development takes place, the male (centrosome) appears as the organizing genius of the process.

15. This process, by which a fertilized germ-cell divides and redivides, and so builds up a "body," is quite similar to that by which a protozoön divides and redivides to form a numerous colony.

16. A 'body' indeed *is* such a colony, coöperatively associated in definite form, of which all the millions of cells are practically continuous with the original fertilized germ, and one with it.

17. Every cell in such a body has apparently the same nuclear elements as the original cell, equally derived from both parents; but is differentiated so far as to be able to fulfil its special part in the body.

18. The process of division of these microscopic cells is strangely exact and complex; and the various elements of the nucleus seem to be themselves divided into two, on each occasion, with strange preciseness.

19. The constituent cells of each race of animals have always a certain number of nuclear threads or chromosomes—fixed for that particular race.

20. When, therefore, a sperm-cell and germ-cell unite, they each first extrude or expel half the number of their chromosomes, so that after union the joint cell is provided again with the precise number of chromosomes characteristic of the race.

21. The exact nature of these 'maturation' divisions and expulsions is far from clear; but it would seem that they are carried out in such a way as, while retaining always the basic elements of the Race, to secure a continual and endless sorting of these into new combinations.

22. These complex evolutions occurring, as described, in the interior of the most primitive cells, look as much like the last results of some far antecedent or invisible operations (of which we know nothing) as like the first commencement of the visible organic world with which we are acquainted.

www.ingramcontent.com/pod-product-compliance
Lightning Source LLC
LaVergne TN
LVHW090856100726
842905LV00054B/397